Kicking the Bla

'Welch's blazing honesty sears the soul, while setting the mind on fire with hope. His poetic insights urge us to live a conscious and caring life. He teaches us to stare down death.'

Marianne McDonald, Professor of Classics and Theatre, MRIA

'Kicking the Black Mamba *bears testimony to the bonds of family that must endure the worst loss, the loss of a child. Robert Welch gives us a roar of a book, rooted in love, heartsore with grief, ending in a magnificent meeting of father and son, a true act of recognition. This is writing to cherish.'*

Frank McGuinness, playwright and poet

'*This is a book about that most terrible of things that can happen to parents: the death of a loved child. The book charts a son's battle with his demons, mostly alcohol. For those who knew this brilliant and tortured young man, Egan's human frailties were matched, in at least equal measure, by his unnatural talents and uncommon intellectual insights as well as by his innate generosity and sense of humour. He was described accurately, by a Sardinian soothsayer, as "good, through and through". The book recounts the desperate attempts of his devoted parents to try to pull him away from death. It is no misery memoir however, because in the end it is a book about the survival of love and of hope.*'

Professor Gerry McKenna,
Retired Vice-Chancellor, University of Ulster

'*A remarkable and painfully honest work describing the efforts of anguished parents to prevent a brilliant son from heartrending tragedy.*'

Colin Smythe, Publisher

POETRY
Muskerry
Secret Societies
The Blue Formica Table
The Evergreen Road
Constanza

FICTION
The Kilcolman Notebook
Groundwork

CRITICISM
Irish Poetry from Moore to Yeats
A History of Verse Translation from the Irish: 1789–1897
Changing States: Transformations in Modern Irish Writing
The Abbey Theatre 1899–1999: Form and Pressure

AS EDITOR
The Oxford Companion to Irish Literature
The Way Back: George Moore
Literature and the Art of Creation (*co-edited with Suheil Bushrui*)
Selected Poems of Patrick Galvin (*co-edited with Greg Delanty*)
W.B. Yeats: Writings on Irish Folklore, Legend and Myth
The Concise Companion to Irish Literature
The Oxford History of the Irish Book (*co-general editor with Brian Walker, 5 volumes*)

DRAMA
Protestants

AS GAEILGE
Tearmann
Japhy Ryder ar Shleasaibh na Mangartan

Kicking the Black Mamba

Life, Alcohol and Death

Robert Anthony Welch

DARTON · LONGMAN + TODD

First published in 2012 by
Darton, Longman and Todd Ltd
1 Spencer Court
140 – 142 Wandsworth High Street
London SW18 4JJ

ISBN 978-0-232-52895-4

A catalogue record for this book is available from the British Library

Phototypeset by Kerrypress Ltd, Luton, Bedfordshire
Printed and bound by ScandBook AB, Sweden

In Memoriam

Egan Anthony Welch

1980 – 2007

Let therefore, O Lord, the same hand which is to receive them then, preserve these soules till (Death); let that mouth, that breath'd them into us, at first, breath always upon them, whilst they are in us, and sucke them into it selfe, when they depart from us. Receive our soules, o Lord, because they belong to thee; and preserve our bodies, because they belong to these soules ... and though thou divide man and wife, mother and child, friend and friend, by the hand of Death, yet stay them that stay, and send them away that goe, with this consolation, that though we part at divers daies, and by divers waies, here, yet wee shall all meet at one place, and at one day, a day that no night shall determine, the day of the glorious Resurrection.

John Donne, Dean of St Paul's Cathedral, from *The Prayer before the Sermon of Commemoration of the Lady Danvers* (1627)

Contents

Contents

Preface

It is normal for a reader to skip the preface and get straight to the book. I ask the reader to stay this impulse on this occasion and look quickly through this brief prologue.

This is a book about the death of my son Egan, by drowning, in January 2007, a death that ended four years of suffering and turmoil, during which he lost his livelihood through the sharp practice of someone he trusted, sank deep into depression, and took to drink for solace. He became an alcoholic and was hospitalised many times as he struggled with his addiction. When he drowned in the River Bann outside Coleraine in Northern Ireland, it was not suicide, as was rumoured at the time. He was drunk and fell into the river, having left a house in the small hours of the morning after a bout of heavy drinking on top of Antabuse, the drug some alcoholics are prescribed to create a physical revulsion against alcohol so they can stop.

A few weeks after Egan died, a friend wrote from India to say that I should try to write about his death. She was certain that a meaning was to be found in this sorrowful life and its sad ending. This book is the result of that prompt. It was a terrifying and exhausting thing to write. I decided not to pull any punches, but to lay bare my own experiences of what it is like to live with and to love an alcoholic, to go through the agony of watching someone decline towards what you know is going to be the outcome, death, unless some transformation of the mind and will intervenes.

I wanted to show the bravery of the fight Egan made against his disease, but he was not to win through, as is the case with so many. I also wanted to show that, somehow, his short life had meaning, and the only way in which I could express that meaning was in religious terms. This is not, emphatically not, a religious book; I do not have the ethical, theological, or moral subtlety or training that would enable me to tackle a religious subject such as this: death and its meaning for life. No, this is a book about experience, the experience of pain Egan underwent and the experience of observing, in terror, the process of sorrow that his mother, Angela, his sister and brothers and I went through as we saw his fate heading towards him. But, as I tried to make sense of these experiences (despair, hope, resolve, anger, love) I found that I turned frequently to the language and ideas of the Gospels and St Paul, especially when it came to describing the mystery of hope and love that lies at the heart of sorrow, the mystery of resurrection. As it says in the Nicene Creed: '*Et expecto resurrectionem mortuorum*' (I await [anticipate] the resurrection of the dead). May it be so, and may we see him again in all his strength and beauty.

This is a book written not for 'therapeutic' reasons: it is a search for meaning in the death of a greatly loved son. It is also written in the hope that the story and the experiences unfolded here will give some consolation to those who have had to go through similar nightmares, or who are currently enduring them.

Robert Anthony Welch
Coleraine, February 2010

Acknowledgements

I wish to thank my family for their love and support during our mutual grief as we mourn Egan. He is deeply loved by Rachel, his sister, and his brothers, Killian and Tiernan. He is mourned by his relations on both sides of the family: Flor and Marian O'Riordan; Richard Dormer; Dominic and Rosalind Welch; Imali Fernando, Marian, Teresa, and Eileen Welch; his grand-uncle Robert Edward Welch; and his cousins.

I want to thank Charlotte Moffett, Egan's beautiful fiancée, who brought such density of colour into his last months. My thanks to the following persons who, in different ways, shared Egan's cross with him: Fr Charles Keaney PP; Fr Ciaran Page; the Reverend Ian McNie; John McConaghey; Gerry Dallat; the members of Bally-money Alcoholics Anonymous; the staff at Cuan Mhuire, Newry, at St John of God's, Dublin, and at the Ross Thomson Unit, Causeway Hospital, Coleraine; James Harley, GP; Jimmy Madden; Brian Harte; Teresa McKenna; Billy Clugston; Roger Cassidy; Patricia and John Noone, and their children, Catherine, Peter, Rosemary and Alison; Pino and Giusi Serpillo; Lee, Pauline, and Anna Nolan; Paddy and Pauline Doogan; Declan Molloy; Michael and Ann Carr; Patrick Durkan; Danny O'Kane; Ryan Johnston; Kieran O'Doherty; Colin Smythe; Gerry and Phil McKenna; Cathy Boyd; John and Alex Pitcher; Glenda and Gregory Wylie; Sophie

Acknowledgements

Hillan and John Edward King; Bruce and Nicky Stewart; Che and John Murphy; Ganesh Devy; Dr Hutchinson, Ballymoney; Andrew and Alison Hadfield; Lyn Moffett; Paddy Butcher; Trevor, Julia and Naomi Smith; the police service of Northern Ireland, especially Paul Meikle; the police divers from Yorkshire who recovered Egan's body; Bann River Rescue.

My thanks to those friends and colleagues at the University of Ulster and its Faculty of Arts whose letters and words meant so much to us in the days and weeks following Egan's death; likewise the staff, volunteers and trustee board of Causeway Citizens Advice Bureau; Derry (A.N.) Jeffares and his wife Jeanne, both no longer with us in this visible world, helped and loved Egan in many practical ways over the years. Ray Leonard, also now among the dead, was an angelic ministering spirit to Egan during dark days. My thanks to David Simpson, head of technical services in the Faculty of Arts at the University of Ulster, for his technical help and generous advice, and to Debbie Mitchell, who assisted when David left to take up a post in the Glasgow School of Art and Design. A special word of thanks to my agent, Jonathan Williams, for his painstaking work on the text; and to James Hogan, who cleared out many irrelevancies and much self-indulgence.

My gratitude and love to the person who knows how deep true sorrow hits – Angela, Egan's mother.

1

Nights in White Satin

I am writing this sitting in a hotel lobby in Derry city. The hotel overlooks the River Foyle. The City Hotel, as it is called, is co-owned by a man called Patrick Durkan, a tall, gentle, considerate accountant, who once froze my blood when he told me that his daughter Deirdre had died in his arms. Patrick is a soft-spoken person who conveys the feeling that he touches things very lightly in a kind of questioning stroke, leaving the faintest, most delicate impression. When he works through my tax returns with me, I see him float lightly over the bundles of invoices and receipts, sifting through the disparate records to produce order, an immaculate and clear bottom line.

Some years ago, Patrick told me one Saturday, sitting in the sun-drenched bar of his hotel, that he was driving his daughters to visit a former schoolteacher. It was winter, the winter before Deirdre was to take her A levels. They had passed through the small farming town of Desertmartin. Just outside the town, at a spot known as Reuben's Glen, heading down a gentle incline, the car hit black ice. It was travelling at no more than thirty or forty miles per hour. The car spun and careered into a field below the road. It came to a halt. There had, he said, been a slight thump as Deirdre's head hit the roof of the car. Patrick was shaken and dizzy, but he was thanking God that things had not been worse: they could have gone in the opposite direction into oncoming traffic; the car had not turned over. Patrick looked to his left and saw that his daughter Mary was fine, amidst the broken glass.

He looked round at Deirdre, who lay still, sprawled on the back seat. He spoke to her but she did not reply. He got out, opened the back door and lifted her from the car. Elizabeth and John Palmer, who lived nearby, came on the scene and got her a blanket to cover her. Patrick hugged her and felt the warmth leave her body. He and Mary prayed for her. She had died instantly.

As I write this, the pop singer Norah Jones is whining her melodramatic woe through the piped music that accompanies breakfast in the hotel. When Patrick told me this harrowing story that brilliant Saturday afternoon in the hotel bar, now at my back and empty, I felt what everyone must do in such circumstances – a mixture of what Aristotle, thousands of years ago called, writing about the effects of tragedy, pity and fear. Pity: the sorrow you feel for someone who has had to go through something terrible; fear: the cold shock of terror that such a thing could happen to you and to those you love. We live exposed to damage, and something in us knows too that life for each one of us is going to involve a version of such an ordeal.

The music shifts, from Norah Jones to The Moody Blues and their great hymn to melancholy from the 1960s, 'Nights in White Satin', its explosions of frantically declared love, the chant at the end of each of the verses that, in the end, all your worst fears will be confirmed and you will be just what you want to be.

The writer Joseph Conrad was, as one would expect of a novelist, preoccupied with character, save that, with Conrad, character acquires a quality of inescapable fate. In *Lord Jim* (1900), his extraordinary story of honour, cowardice, and shame, Conrad writes that a person's fate is ordained from the start, as if inscribed in stone. Lord Jim, who has been involved in an act of collective cowardice, when the entire crew of a ship saved themselves by leaving behind their human cargo of pilgrims in a foundering boat (which in fact fails to sink), hopes he can wipe the slate of his guilt clean. This, says Marlow – Conrad's storyteller in the novel – is a delusion. It is futile to strive against what we are, old Marlow says after many years wandering the high seas, and to try to do so is to behave foolishly, 'as if the initial word of each of our destiny were not graven in imperishable characters upon the face of a rock.' That is to say: the compulsion is there, right from the outset, to accomplish your own particular fate, whatever that may be, but whatever it turns out to be, it will involve disaster as much as triumph. Indeed, Conrad would say, the strong likelihood will be that the scales will dip towards the side of tragedy. This explains the powerful reverberations of the melancholy in 'Nights in White Satin': you are impelled by your nature to become what you will end up being in the end, and that, as often as not, involves sadness and disaster. Or so it is without some other sort of intervention. This moral fatalism of Conrad is a quality he found deeply engrained in English life and culture, and you find it too in, of all places (I know, it's an odd juxtaposition) The Moody Blues, or Nick Drake. It was one of the reasons, I think, why this Polish mariner became a great English novelist: he knew, from the core, the sorrow of England, its sense of doom.

I started writing this memoir in a notebook bought for me by my son Egan, who was drowned on 28 January 2007. It is now 7 April of the same year, a little over two months since his death, less than two months since he was buried in St John's churchyard in Coleraine. It took them eleven days to recover the body. The notebook in which I write is bound in beautiful soft blue leather. It is, we are told on the back in lettering stamped into the surface, made in Italy by Francesco Lionetti; and inside the front cover, on the flyleaf, is a message from the maker, which says: 'We hope you enjoy this product made by Florentine Artisans using the best quality of leather.' The paper is thick and parchment-like in colour, and it takes the wet flow of the fountain pen cleanly, no blemishes soaking through to the other side.

The spine of this beautiful notebook is marred by four cuts or tears in the leather, which expose the brown hide beneath the tooled nap. I am not certain how these cuts got here. Egan bought this notebook for me in November 2006. Angela, his mother, was with him when he did so. They often went shopping together in TK Maxx in Coleraine, a discount designer warehouse where he spotted this notebook and, knowing that I have a thing about note-books, bought it, intending to give it to me for Christmas. He found a use for it before then.

Late that November Egan tried to kill himself and he used this notebook to write down exactly what he did on the morning of his attempted suicide. I am now going to quote, from the opening pages of this notebook, Egan's meticulous account of his actions and state of mind on the morning when he tried to take his own life.

Dear Mum and Dad

What I have I have deemed incurable; worse, chronic

Facts: 11.27
I am entirely sober and have just prepared a lethal cocktail of propranolol + diazepam which will over the hours hopefully kill me and put an end to our miseries caused by my illness. Otherwise I'll end up with severe renal damage and add to your probs!...

If I die
It is not alcohol that killed me, its something else? I'm sober now (after 4 days) but I think its time for my first drink. Did you know that the toxic dose of propranolol is 1g. Let me put that in perspective, one tablet is at most 80mg. Similarly did you know that you would have to take 1600 5mg diazepam tablets at least in order to achieve toxicity.

Killing yourself therefore is not easy. I avoided coffee this morning so my heart will slow to a lethal rate. I have taken the first of three ground up glasses of valium approx 1000 mg and roughly 0.9g of propranolol, also ground up in a pestle and mortar.

I love all of you

I hate hurting you.

It is my belief, although of course I cannot be certain, that the four cuts on the spine of this notebook were caused by Egan biting into it after he had written these terrible words, so full of sorrow and of love.

This was the third time Egan had attempted to kill himself, although the other occasions were, possibly, in that worn and inadequate phrase, cries for help (as if a cry for help could be anything other than a scream of desperation if it takes such an extreme form). By November 2006 Egan had moved into his own house round the corner from us, which Angela and I had helped him to buy, and he was living there with his girlfriend, a beautiful girl called Charlotte Moffett. Charlotte had known Egan since she was about twelve or so, and had loved him, she told Angela, since then; that is, she had held him steadfast in her heart for more than ten years. As a young teenager, she was in the same school as Egan and his brother Tiernan. Tiernan, our youngest, she knew slightly better than Egan, being closer in age to him, and on the way home from the Dominican Convent in Portstewart, she would tag along with Tiernan as her way of being in the company of Egan, whose good looks, she has said, would cut to her heart whenever she saw him. They had taken up together and she was astonished that things had fallen out this way. She later told Angela , when Egan was dead, that she would wake up in the morning and look at him beside her and think: I can't believe this; the man I've always loved is here beside me. Charlotte was working in a pharmacy before going back to university to resume her studies in pharmacology; Egan had begun to study towards a degree in basic science at the Open University. They planned to get married once she had graduated.

On the day of his third suicide attempt, Charlotte had stayed the night before at her mother's house in Portstewart and was going to work around one o'clock at the pharmacy in Asda. He had told her not to bother coming by the house on her way to work, which she would normally do if she were leaving from her mother's, since, he said, he would probably be working on his Open University coursework. But she did come by, to find the door locked from the inside. She had a key, but Egan had left his key in the lock inside, so that Charlotte could not get her key into the lock outside. The blinds were drawn, so she could not see in. Charlotte was also a bit self-conscious: Egan's house on Brook Street gave directly on to the pavement and there was no privacy. Turning back to the front door,

Charlotte tried, once again, to push her key into the lock and found that this time—amazingly—her key pushed his out and she was able to unlock the door.

Charlotte found Egan on the sofa and knew he wasn't right. His speech was slurred and he looked dazed. She called Angela on her mobile phone and told her that there was something funny about Egan; she said she didn't think he was drunk but he was almost incoherent. This was a Saturday and Angela and I were at home, having lunch. Angela had left her phone upstairs, so we did not hear it ringing. (Charlotte did not have our landline number.) Meanwhile, Egan was drifting in and out of consciousness. During one half-lucid interval Charlotte asked him what our landline number was and he slurred it out. Then he said, no, that wasn't it, but Charlotte rang it anyway and got through. He was trying to stop her, confused and all as he was, from making contact with us, attempting to spare us the pain and agony.

Angela called the ambulance, telling the person she spoke to what she could about what had happened from her brief conversation with Charlotte. She was told to get Egan on to his side. Angela explained that she wasn't actually with Egan at the time but that his fiancée was, so she rang Charlotte's mobile, and, using both phones, she passed on to Charlotte the advice she was getting from the ambulance on the landline.

By now I had that feeling I always got during Egan's bouts of distress. As well as his attempts to kill himself, there had been dozens of other similar situations: panics; car drives in numbed silence as we responded to a call from Egan or someone else wondering what it was we were to face this time; long hours of waiting in the Accident & Emergency unit while Egan was examined, then sedated; waiting for news as to whether or not he was to be admitted to hospital, or (more often than not) sent home with no one to look after him except us; attempting to clean his flat in Ballymoney (where he lived for a time) as he staggered around in his filthy dressing gown, trying to pretend he had not been drinking; crazed phone calls from some pub or other where he had fallen in with a gang of thugs he was convinced were going to kill him (something that could easily have happened on a number of occasions); and so on. Anyone who has tried to look after an alcoholic will be familiar with such instances, and worse.

*   *   *

I began writing this in the lobby of the City Hotel in Derry. It is now a few weeks later and I am continuing the account in our small house in Co. Donegal, a stone-built gamekeeper's cottage built in the 1880s on a wild mountainside in Leamagowra, between Ardara and Glencolumcille. Egan has stayed here many times with us from when he was aged about eleven and he helped us renovate it, assisting me, for example, when I hacked off all the lime plaster from the interior walls. I recall his face grey with lime-dust, smiling, laughing with his friend Che who used to come down for the fun of it. One time, he and Che, in the frantic hopes and expectations of late childhood, began to try to rebuild the old police barrack beside the cottage, which had been burned out by the IRA in the Irish War of Independence. This hope of reconstruction, in outright defiance of the futility of the task, is a kind of summary of Egan's life. There is a gaping window in the ruined barrack, built out of poured mass concrete, which Egan and Che tried to repair using bits of stone, brick, sand and cement they got from the workmen who were renovating the house. I didn't have the heart to stop them. And now, when I am in Donegal, I sometimes go down to the barrack and look out the empty square rectangle of the vanished window, put my hand on their pathetic masonry and think of the constant blazing renewal of the fire of hope in us, generation after generation, in spite of all.

I have just come in having walked down to close the front gate which has blown open in the harsh April winds. Walking back up the rough drive, shadowed by the old pine trees that were planted here not long after the cottage was built, I got that ancient smell of the freshening pine needles renewing themselves for another year. The smell brings back memories of my young manhood when my friends and I would set off on exploratory visits to West Cork and Kerry, into the Gaeltacht, looking for meaning in the old trees, the mossy smells, the stone-built houses in remote mountains, clear streams, well-water, flagstones outside the houses leading to the aromatic secrecies of a hay-filled outbuilding. And up in the hills, auburn, peat-stained water flowing over granite. We were trying to connect into something venerable and old, as the young do. Irish became a magic language, full of powerful resonance. And the smell of the pine needles, that resinous persistence, carries an intimation that something may be revealed, something true, which will connect the urgency of how you feel, now, in the given moment, to sedimented layers of instinct and knowledge. This smell mixes the ancientness of autumn with the fiery hope of spring in a confused and blissful ambiguity.

That scent of pine resin and needles – its mixture of hope and sadness – is something that Egan will never again experience, at least not the way in which we experience their interactions in this world. Or, maybe not. This is a book I have undertaken to write to try to tell Egan's story from the point of view of someone who loved him, and for whom there remains always the lingering hope – a longing that at times expands into laborious, unsettled conviction – of a resurrection; so that there yet may be a time and a place where he will again, with me, get the smell of pine-resin in the air on a spring day washed and freshened by mountain wind and rain.

When I pulled up outside Egan's house in Brook Street on that day in November 2006 after he had taken his 'lethal cocktail' (lethal was a favourite word of his), the ambulance crew was taking him out on a stretcher. I saw his face, as grey as the water of the Bann on an overcast day. He was unconscious and had the look of death.

We say of things that we fear may work out badly, though we may not have enough evidence to be certain of failure, that we have 'misgivings' – a strange and wonderful word. There is a phrase— 'my heart misgives'— used in Marlowe, Shakespeare and Milton, indicating that something which is feared is in the offing. This was why, perhaps, there was more than just sympathy and fellow-feeling involved when Patrick Durkan told me how he had held his dying, then dead, daughter in his arms outside Desertmartin. When he told me this, we were having a pint in the hotel bar. The television was on. Ireland and France were playing in the Six Nations rugby tournament. It was First Communion day, so the bar and lobby was thronged with people, the little girls resplendent in their white frocks and lace veils, the mothers done up to the nines in their glad rags, stilettos, short skirts, the works; the men in good suits and ties or in expensive casual wear. And in the midst of all this festive clamour, a father's sorrowful face sunk to his chest as he told his story.

Patrick's skin was pale in the brilliant light flooding in through the plate glass windows, sparkling on the ashtrays and the chromium supports of the high leather stools on which we were sitting. As he told me how he had held his daughter in his arms my heart misgave, as in Milton's phrase from *Paradise Lost*, when he tells us how Adam's did before he took the apple from Eve. I was destined to go through something of the same order of experience as Patrick had. I somehow knew then that some such ordeal lay ahead.

2

From the VIP Lounge to Gethsemane

I left Angela at the hospital Accident & Emergency unit where they had taken Egan. Charlotte had gone to work in the pharmacy. We arranged to meet up in the Asda supermarket across the road once I'd collected Rachel, our daughter and eldest child, from the train. Rachel, living in Belfast, was coming to stay for a day or two, mostly to see Egan, to whom she was very close.

Angela, it was arranged, would ring me when Egan was settled and all three of us would go and visit him later, along with Charlotte. Angela had planned to go shopping with Rachel at TK Maxx, a ritual excursion every time she visited us. When I collected Rachel and told her what had happened, she wanted to go to the hospital immediately. There was no point, I told her; all we could do was sit and wait in A & E. Better to wait for word from her mother. She should go along to TK Maxx and I would ring her if there was any news.

This may seem a little odd, callous even, but the fact of the matter is that the attempted suicides, shattering as they were, were not that different in their emotional turbulence and shock, for us at least, from the necessary rescues of Egan from bedrooms, flats and various pubs over the previous three years. We had become used to distress, to Egan's raving sorrow and rage, to dreadful things happening. We had seen his body subjected to abuse and hurt, both self-inflicted and inflicted by others. On one occasion, for instance, we had to call the fire brigade to get him down from the attic in our garage where he had gone to drink, in a single afternoon, what turned out to be three bottles of neat vodka. I had to call the emergency services because I realised I would not be able to get him down the rickety ladder single-handed. Such experiences meant that we had become resigned to the unrelenting imminence of shock in our lives, which could be counted upon to recur with steady frequency. To put it crudely, a suicide attempt was like more of the same, in that the kind of drinking Egan went in for was in itself a form of unremitting self-destruction. But this time it turned out to be different.

I had not, at this stage, discovered the blue notebook containing his suicide message and his description of the 'lethal cocktail'. So when Angela called me to say that she had been told to stay at the hospital because Egan was in serious danger, I was not prepared. Angela was told that he might not make it. She asked me to come to the hospital immediately. My problem now was that Rachel was in the town, shopping. I called her and she answered the phone while at the check-out counter at TK Maxx. She ran up the streets to where I was parked, at the corner of a busy and dangerous junction on one of the arterial roads that lead into Coleraine's nightmare one-way system. Eventually I saw her, weighed down with those outsize bags they issue in discount stores. She got into the car out of breath and horror-struck at what I had told her on the phone. We drove in stricken silence to the hospital.

Egan had, by now, been moved into the cardiac unit. We were shown into a side-room off the treatment area, where Angela was sitting. The waiting room had the grim aspect such places of sorrow and anxiety have. There was a shower and toilet: it was possible to stay overnight. There was a Teasmade with plastic cups and those small tubs of artificial milk lidded with detachable strips. The chairs were of the wipe-clean sort with grey polyurethane upholstery that exhaled when you sat down on it.

When sad things are in their courses, people who undergo them often say afterwards that, while going through what they had to go through, they felt unreal. There is something in this. I felt unreal in that waiting room with those terrible chairs. But this doesn't really take you to the fiery burning marrow of the way it is at such moments. There is a slowing down of time; there is an expansion of fear and tension. Objects acquire a cumbersome obtrusiveness, as if they are incubating what could break out at any moment: pure threat. Colours fade to a slack and reluctant differentiation. There is a sense of futility, and also boredom. You are there because your son is in danger of losing his life and yet you wish to be almost anywhere else. And intertwined with this there is a small, tiny muted rage of resentment, not so much against Egan (although there is a trace of this too) but against all those circumstances of failure, self-indulgence and indifference that have brought him and you together in this place; he in the cardiac unit, you in that grim little room.

The doctor, a quietly spoken, concerned Indian, comes in. He sits down, meticulously riffles through his notes, and then tells us that Egan is 'flatlining', that is, his heart rate is so low as to register on the screen monitor as a flat line. At times, he says, the heart seems to be stopping. However, it then starts up again and Egan begins to writhe on the bed, tearing at the various drips and attachments. The doctor is going to call in an anaesthetist to tranquillise Egan in order to get him through the trauma of the overdose.

Afterwards Egan told us that, before he was anaesthetised, he saw weird things, among them four horsemen riding towards him, while he was on foot, cowering in fear that they would trample over him.

We are shown into a room closer to the cardiac unit and can now hear, clearly, Egan's intermittent howls of agony and fear as the poison of the drugs works through his system. John Kernahan, the anaesthetist, is a tall, dark-haired man in his early thirties wearing a light green surgical gown. He has the height and natural command of a hurler or Gaelic footballer. He is a northerner from the country somewhere, possibly North Antrim. He tells us that the medics have been unable to sedate Egan. 'Nothing is touching him', he says. 'I will have to put him under with a general anaesthetic. He may not come-to for three days. It is the only way they can work on him'.

Although the anaesthetist is not saying that Egan is out of danger, he gives a very clear sense that the outlook is not necessarily as bad as we had first been given to understand. Meanwhile, John Kernahan tells us that there are only three ventilators (life-support machines) at Causeway Hospital and all three are in use. One man had a severe asthma attack and there were two other young men, apart from Egan, who had tried to kill themselves that night. What is going on? What drives young men into the kind of despair that leads to suicide or to the kind of reckless disregard for personal safety that it is almost the same thing?

Some years before all this, Egan's closest friend, Guy Harper, was beaten to death outside Kelly's Nightclub in Portrush. Kelly's is the top night-spot in Northern Ireland, and one of the major venues for the young (by which I mean teenagers between thirteen and eighteen: if you're older than that, then Kelly's is considered too juvenile for you). It attracts celebrity DJs who charge thousands of pounds a night to appear: personages with names like Lisa Lashes, or Yellow Hammer. Rappers come, hip-hoppers, famous mixers of house music, and so on. They often fly in from London by helicopter, land on the helipad overlooking the wild Causeway coast, go into the VIP lounge, have a good time, do the gig, and then return to London that same night at three or four in the morning. The place, in spite of elaborate security, has acquired a certain notoriety. There have been a number of large drug seizures at Kelly's and there have been killings. One involved a girl who was given one of those rape drugs; she was then carried out by the young man who had spiked her drink past the bouncers at the door (who presumably thought: here is another kid legless from alcohol or Ecstasy), driven, unconscious, to Portstewart Strand where she was raped and then murdered.

Another victim was Guy Harper, who was killed in March 2001. At this time, Egan was working as a web designer at the university in the School of Biomedical Sciences, where he and a young and ambitious lecturer, Clive Mulholland, had set up a virtual version of the school, offering a master's degree via the internet. But Egan, by now, had also started up his own company, Twelfth Dimension Design, specialising in graphic design and animated websites. At that time such expertise was still a rarity. Egan was doing incredibly well in his own business and had already started to employ people, including an experienced business manager. He was making lots of money: in the first year alone he made something in the region of £60,000 clear profit. The new company's most lucrative contract was the one he had negotiated himself: the all-singing, all-dancing website for Kelly's.

On a Saturday night in March 2001 Egan was working late on Kelly's website. He and Guy were intending to go on to the nightclub. Egan rang Guy when he had finished working and said he was taking a taxi to Portrush and would meet him there. Guy pointed out that it was very late. The clocks had gone forward that evening which Egan hadn't realised. He said he would go to Portrush anyway and got out of the taxi at Guy's house. Joel, Guy's father, for the first time in his life, drove his son to Kelly's. He had never done so before because he didn't want him going there.

When they entered the club, they separated for a while, each mixing with different groups of people. Then it appears that Egan decided to leave and asked Guy if he wanted to go to Portstewart with him. Guy said he would stay on.

The following morning a knock came on our door at about seven o'clock. The police. Guy Harper was in intensive care at the hospital; he was in a bad way and it was not looking good. They understood Egan was with him the night before. Could they speak with him? We told the police that Egan had not come home the previous night, in itself not an unusual thing: he would often spend the night at Guy's or with other friends in the Triangle. The police could not tell us very much about what had happened other than that Guy had been set upon by a gang on his way home from Kelly's and had been so badly beaten and kicked that his life was in danger. The police had been given Egan's name because they had been seen together for a time at Kelly's. We were now in a panic. Where was Egan? Angela rang his mobile which started to ring on our kitchen range. He hadn't taken it with him.

There was an hour or more of tension. Angela rang the hospital to enquire about Guy and was told he was not good. She asked if there was another young man, Egan, also in the hospital. The nurse she spoke to didn't think so, but said that it was the switch-over time for day and night staff and she would ask a daytime nurse to ring us in half an hour. A nurse did indeed ring and confirmed that Egan was not in the hospital, neither as a patient or a visitor. Angela kept ringing Egan's department at the university and at 9 a.m. the phone was answered. She was relieved to hear his voice. He knew nothing about what had happened to Guy. Egan left the university, met up with his mother, went to the police station where he made a statement about the time he had been in Guy's company. As he was leaving the station the CID man who had been dealing with the case said: 'Despite all our hard work, those people will be out again in two years'. 'Please don't say that,' said Egan. The CID man was proved to have been correct.

Egan rang the hospital frequently to ask about Guy but he got the same answer every time – that Guy was critically ill. Angela went into work but couldn't concentrate, and decided to visit. Joel Harper, Guy's father, was there. Angela told Joel that Egan had said that, if he had been with Guy, this wouldn't have happened. Joel's response was that if Egan had been outside Kelly's in that mayhem, there would have been two young men on life-support machines, not one.

This sorrow within a sorrow does not end here. Joel vowed (it was printed in the local papers) that if Guy's killers ever got out, he would kill them himself. One or two of them did get out, within a couple of years, and Joel of course realised he could not do what he had said he would do in the madness of grief. These young thugs, when they got out, were sauntering around the Triangle, half-proud of what they had done, enjoying the reputation.

The motive for this killing was never really made clear. There had been an altercation in the bar in Kelly's between Guy and these young men; Guy, it would appear, made up to one of the girls that were with them; they were asked to leave, and then they just set upon Guy with brutal ferocity, the girls joining in.

One night, after two or three of those involved in the killing had been released, Joel was out drinking with a couple of friends in Portrush after a game of golf. All normal. They broke up at around midnight in the Harbour Bar, a pub maintained to retain the authentic squalor of a place resorted to by sea-salt types, and near the fishing boats, sea-walls and cliffs. Joel announced to his friends that he was going to take a turn before heading back to Gladys, his wife. He set off on his own. Nobody was driving because they had all had a fair skinful that night. Joel went missing and did not return. The following day a man's body was found on the rocks beneath Ramore Head, behind the harbour. A cliff walk runs from the harbour up around the Head. There are many dangerous turns, vertiginous falls. The body was Joel's. At his funeral a few days later, I read from St Paul and shouldered the coffin for a few paces, as did Egan. When he stepped from under the oak casket, he looked at me and said, spelling out each word: *I'll not forget that.*

Egan never got over Guy's murder and Joel's death. They were related, of course, and Egan regarded himself as implicated in these two deaths, even in some way a catalyst for them. It was as if he felt that his absence from Guy's side when he was attacked had set off a course of events that would lead to his own attempted suicides and his death. This is not rational, but that is beside the point: what matters is how someone feels. And my son felt everything, blamed himself for misfortunes that befell others. He did not, like so many do, *play* at emotions. He *had* them. His feeling capacity had the total purity of a saint. Many of us dispose our emotions according to a calculation that we make in which our own advantage gets figured in. There was not a trace of that in Egan.

What is it that drives so many young men to suicide or to putting themselves in situations of danger? Is it the case that nature, what Shakespeare called 'great creating nature'— the form and energy that drives the universe— has decided that the numbers of males now in existence are surplus to requirements? She does not need their strength any more in the fields or in the factories throughout the developed world. Such qualities are still needed in what we call the Third World, but in such countries endurance, skill and male physical prowess are most often necessary tools in the creation of wealth for a world that grows ever more merciless and exploitative. Where is the dignity of labour in the miserable conditions endured by those poor wretches who work sixteen-hour shifts in the gem pits of Sri Lanka? They are lowered by ropes down three-foot wide shafts to a depth of some forty feet; they then, by the light of candles, crawl along tunnels that have been scraped out by hand, every inch of their clothes and bodies soaking wet from the water that continually seeps from the earthen walls; they claw the sides of the shaft, seeking the hard, embedded particles that may be precious stones, while at the far end of the man-made cave other men tear farther into the muddy clay. Baskets attached to ropes carry the wet earth to the surface where it is sluiced through with the water that the gimcrack petrol-driven pumps suck up from the shafts. This washing through the grit, searching for the diamonds, is carried out by women. Only men are capable of the work down below. After such appalling effort, what alternative can there be for many of these men but the oblivion of cheap arrack, the local hooch; not unlike the relief from slog, contempt and sadness that drink gave the Irish navvies who built the great British motorways of the 1960s, but a gulf of indignity and powerlessness extends between those unhappy Irishmen who shovelled concrete in the English cold and rain, and the comfortless misery endured by the gem-pit workers. These creatures are the exhausted muscles, nerves, and sinews that the world market compels to its relentless search for what can be traded in order that those who exercise this force can live in a sensuous haze of continuous desire and never-to-be-sated arousal.

Such are the uses now for male strength. Is it the case that young men are becoming aware that nature is beginning not to have a use for them as they are or have been, and that, coming into that awareness unconsciously, they begin to find ways of self-disposal? This is perhaps what Egan tried to do that Saturday in November 2006. Why trouble people whom you love, and whose love for you is a curse to them, any more than is necessary when it is not certain that there is any use for you in a world of heartless force and brute necessity?

At the cardiac unit, John Kernahan explained to us that, because there wasn't a ventilator for Egan he would be transferred to the Antrim Area where a bed was available, and the necessary equipment. He reassured us that the Causeway Hospital nurses who had been looking after Egan would travel in the ambulance with him. His concern was evident and he spoke to us as if the only life that mattered to him was Egan's.

In the vestibule off the unit where they were stabilising our son, a young woman was waiting, seated: jeans, blonde hair, fair skin, exuding an air of wholesomeness and cleanliness. Her husband had had a bad asthma attack, but she has been told he would be fine. When she asked what brought us there, we told her and her face altered as she began to comprehend the horror of other people's lives. She was upset, and this kind of spontaneous sympathy that surfaces continuously was a reminder to a bleak misanthropist like me that human feeling can still occur, that love and kindness are as wired into us as the other, darker, impulses.

Dr Kernahan came back, his white surgical shoes almost soundless on the plastic membrane floor. He said we could go in to see Egan now that he was sedated and stable. The crisis was, for the moment, over. Our son would come round in the next few days; it would take that long for the body to recover from the shock of the lethal dosage and the subsequent anaesthetic.

We went in. The distance between the automatic doors and the trolley bed on which Egan was lying seemed great. The large space was empty but for the single bed, beside which were stands with plastic sachets of medication and sedative hanging from them, transparent tubes going from the rucked base of the sacks into his arms and stomach. Across his mouth was a black mask connected by a ringed and grooved tube to the life-support machine which was breathing for him. We heard the panting inhalations and exhalations of the apparatus and could see his chest rise and fall beneath the flimsy green shift they had put on him. His face was grey, his eyes and mouth encrusted with hardened discharges.

Mostly we live our lives according to convenience. Whenever we opt for a certain course of action, as distinct from some other, it is more often than not because it is convenient. There is a job; someone perhaps puts us in the way of it and the next thing you know you have been in it for forty years because it has been convenient not to stray from the given path. A woman, a man, comes along and wanders into your life. You hang around together.

There is an expectation that something will come of this; you get married, have children. It's convenient. Someone asks you to do something malicious at work; make a disaster of someone else's life. You carry it out, even though you harbour a suspicion that the judgement out of which the suggestion comes may be faulty. But it's too irksome to question the expectation; you do what is required. Someone greatly wrongs or injures someone who matters to you; it is too inconvenient to feel too much because if you did, the nature of the revenge to be exacted is not permissible, cannot be accomplished without self-damage, so you let it lie. You trundle along, a bag of undemanding avoidances, swollen with compliance.

And then someone like Egan comes into your life, an utter inconvenience. And you learn that if there is anything remotely real about the action of love, then this is what it means: inconvenience, being put out. And you resent it too because you are set completely off track. If this new reality is to be coped with, you need to accept that a different set of arrangements is involved: routines are changed, attitudes have to shift, a different experience of time is introduced; you find out what the phrase 'hoping against hope' means in all its searing actuality and pain. You cannot retract what it has become necessary to expend; or at least you could, but if you were to do so, you would know that you add up to nothing more than a worthless bundle of impulses and cravings.

A shark does what a shark does; it has been programmed for millennia to carry out certain functions in response to certain stimuli. A slug emits from its tissue the slime that allows it to traverse the distance from one impulse to another. Each creature has its own unalterable laws of integrity governed by the drives and necessities encoded in its cellular make-up. What a shark does not do, what a slug does not do, is make declarations of fealty to a person or a thing which may then be revoked if the sustaining of that vow becomes an inconvenience. It is only our species that is capable of betrayal, but that makes us also capable of love.

Looking at my son's racked body on the trolley bed in the Coleraine cardiac unit, I realise that this is an inconvenience that is not to be avoided. It is a cross that must be carried. Egan is my own personal version of Christ; someone whom I had always known it would become necessary for me to meet. I am also certain that he surfaces in every person's life and not once but many times. I recall staring, as a child in Friars Road in Cork, at a picture of the Sacred Heart of Jesus on the wall above my bed and waiting, indeed willing, for something transformative to happen. It was a picture of Christ, hands extended in a gesture of merciful compassion, his chest open to reveal a heart encircled by thorns, the spikes cutting into the red and bloody flesh, the eyes raised both in despair and ecstasy to a heaven above the top rail of the picture. And there I was, aged nine or so, waiting for something to happen, wanting to feel. There was nothing. For a long while I thought this meant that the whole God-thing was a dead duck for me. My school mates seemed to have a very strong personal experience of comfort and consolation in prayer and in going to Mass and Holy Communion but, for me, these were meaningless motions. It took me a long while to come to understand that, in my case, Christ could be realised only in the form of human relations, in the experience of what I can only call love, when that love becomes an inconvenience and a cross. I think I can say this with reasonable certainty: that I never properly understood what love meant and what it costs until I saw the suffering Egan went through.

I want to say this as simply as possible. I was shown the actuality of Christ in what Egan went through; he was the means whereby the reality of love was revealed to me, in the fullest possible clarity of realisation. I know now that there had been many other instances where the actuality of Christ was there for me to see if I had had the eyes to see it, but here was the instance where the full implication, in all its shocking detail, unfolded itself.

I am sure this is the meaning of that passage in chapter 25 of the Gospel according to Matthew where Christ says to his disciples that he was hungry and they didn't feed him, he was thirsty and they gave him not to drink; and they say, no, not so, whenever did we deny you anything? And his reply is that whenever they turned their backs on a wretch in the street, stinking of mire and filth, asking for money for a drink, *that* was when they turned away from him, because Jesus is to be found among the wrecks, the engrimed, the disgraced, the prostitutes – in those places where most of us do not wish to go, being places of great embarrassment and inconvenience. The American novelist and storyteller Flannery O'Connor has a phrase that evokes this kind of Christ presence, a haunting human reminder at the edge of things: '[a] ragged figure who moves from tree to tree in the back of the mind'.

He was there in Egan under the anaesthetic, quiet for a while, his ravaged face relaxed, a machine doing his breathing for him.

3

The Rack of this Rough World

That night the hospital team moved Egan to Antrim Area Hospital, a vast medical metropolis on the outskirts of the small county town. Angela, Rachel and I went home and got something to eat and drink. I cannot remember what we ate, but I know that I craved alcohol.

There is a question that lies at the heart of my relationship with Egan and my involvement in and with his illness. Has my drinking, and the drinking culture I created in the house as our children grew up, been a factor in Egan's disastrous experience with alcohol? The answer to this question has to be yes: my drinking habits created an environment in which an alcoholic could thrive. Of course this book is, to a degree, about me as well as being about my son, but its chief intent is to try to see what purpose his life served, and to attempt to achieve this by an accumulation of evidence: of his capacity to endure and to suffer, and the limitlessness of his love. Part of that evidential base has to be my own relationship with drink, my experience of its allure, my admission of the sorrow it can create.

Egan started drinking early, about as early as I had done. My first real drink (as distinct from little tasters of sherry at Christmas when I was a child) was in Kilmallock, County Limerick. I was about fourteen. The secondary school I attended, Coláiste Chríost

Rí (The College of Christ the King) in Cork city, had won through to the schools' Munster Final in hurling. This was a big thing.

Kilmallock, although a small country town, was a place everyone in Ireland had heard of at this time, in 1962. A man had battered his wife to death in a flat there. The newspapers had covered the trial in great detail and the particulars of the violence were the topic of long conversations in our kitchen at home, where my mother and her three sisters would gather in the evenings (when their husbands were on shift work) to have tea, smoking the untipped cigarettes of the time, and complain – mostly about men and their ridiculous habits. For a good while the Kilmallock murder dominated their exchanges. At times they would agree what a beagle (a favourite word of abuse) the husband was but they would also say that she, the wife, had it coming to her with her carry-on: she had had an affair with someone (or so the husband believed) and the killing was, it appeared, to some extent a crime of passion.

So when we walked up the main street of Kilmallock in the grey, frosty air of a winter's day we were all aware that we were in a place where something uncontrollable had taken place, where someone had walked and breathed who was almost certainly destined for the fires of hell. Although an entire posse of our teachers had been sent along to keep an eye on us and to ensure good order, none of them were to be seen, either lay or religious. At that time there was a huge increase in the demand for secondary education, a challenge taken up by religious orders, such as the Christian and Presentation Brothers, orders of laymen who had taken vows of poverty, chastity and obedience, and who lived in communities. They were founded in the nineteenth century to provide a Catholic education when the penal laws were still in force and, as the century wore on, their role was crucial in training young men from the working and farming classes in Ireland so that they could take advantage of the opportunities education could bring. In the 1960s these teaching orders played a key role in providing mass education at a low cost for a new, changing and modern Ireland. There were still, at this time, large numbers of Brothers who taught, but they were now increasingly joined by lay teachers who worked in the religious schools and who shared, to a greater or lesser degree, their Catholic ethos. Our school was a Presentation Brothers school.

As we walked up the main street in Kilmallock that day, it was the opinion of Barry Long, the leader of our small pack of four, that our teachers were off having a few pints and sandwiches before the game. I have no doubt that he was right: they would be comfortably installed in a hotel lounge, sat round a low table in front of a blazing fire, sinking their canines into soft white bread and luscious sandwiches of tangy Limerick ham and thickly sliced tomatoes, washed down by large draughts of bitter, smoky Guinness. All talking Munster Irish: ours was what was known as an 'A' school, where subjects were taught, wherever possible, through Irish. Many of us had been enthralled by the language and would talk in Irish amongst ourselves in the playground as well as taking part in the debates that ran every Friday evening in the school (and you would have thought young men would have other things on their minds at the end of the week), again, all conducted in Irish.

In Kilmallock, however, we were not talking Irish, which Barry Long would have considered not the thing to do. Longy was a tall red-haired fellow with a languid stride, white skin and an air of complete confidence. He was quietly spoken, though his language was foul. His school black trousers were drainpipe narrow on his long legs; he wore black winkle-pickers with long pointed toes; and his school tie was wrenched into the tiniest knot possible to make it look like what was known as a Slim Jim, which the Teddy boys had brought into fashion. Longy managed to get away with wearing his hair at Beatle-like shoulder length, even though he was always being told by the Brothers to have it cut.

With us too were Jack Crowley and Dermot Crowley (not related) and we were all smoking. Suddenly, Longy says that we should get a drink. Weren't the teachers at it? We turned down a side street into a pub where we were the only customers and we had no difficulty getting served, in spite of our school blazers and ties and our being obviously well under the legal age of eighteen. Longy asked for Guinness, as did one of the Crowleys; I asked for cider, the other Crowley following suit. I should say, by the way, that at least two of us – me included – had, before entering the pub, taken the precaution of removing from our lapels the heart-shaped badge, mounted on a long brass pin, of the Pioneer Total Abstinence Association, which sat alongside the round gold *fáinne* each of us wore, indicating an advanced prowess in spoken Irish. The *fáinne* stayed in, the Pioneer pin came out and was stuck in the rear of the lapel, so we wouldn't reveal ourselves as the shiftless hypocrites we were. The Pioneer pin was a sign of the pledge each of us had taken at Confirmation that we would abstain from all alcoholic drink until at least the age of eighteen, and offer up this sacrifice for the forgiveness of sins, especially those committed under the influence of drink. Drink, I knew from the conversations round the fire at home, had been a factor in the sexual disorder and murder in this very town. Putting the Pioneer pin under the lapel was a device resorted to not only by boys our age; it was also practiced by grown men who pretended to be teetotallers to their wives or mothers while sloping off to the pub for a quick one, the pin tucked neatly into the nap behind the lapel.

I asked for cider because my father used to love it on a hot day. He had a lip for the drink. So did I; so too did Egan, and there was a drinking culture in our house. There was one occasion when some-thing Egan did rang alarm bells. He was aged sixteen. On the door of our kitchen in Portstewart, Egan had pinned up a series of cartoon pictures, drawn in comic-book style on a single page of lined copybook paper. The opening frame showed a young man in a bar, standing in front of a counter, the bottles ranged behind; the next showed him with friends at the bar, but now with many glasses before them; the third frame had the gaggle of them staggering about the street; next the young man vomiting; then, him seated on the toilet, knees trembling, the trembling indicated by a series of curved lines drawn above each kneecap; and lastly the first box repeated and the whole thing starting off again. This depiction of the repetitious self-hurt caused by alcohol was prophetic, as if Egan had an insight, even at this stage, into what would cut short his life, what he was going to have to undergo: the iron lock of compulsive behaviour, the prison of addiction.

Here was Egan, now twenty-six, at Antrim Hospital, sedated after his third suicide attempt, in horrific actualisation of the lurid crudity of the comic-book drawing set up on our yellow kitchen door to give us all a laugh. It was no laughing matter now.

Angela, Rachel and I set off for Antrim the following morning. We went to intensive care. The unit is a large one. There are protocols to be followed; you have to sign yourself in and wash your hands before visits. There is the sound of life-support machines breathing, their loud hisses of exhalation and inhalation; the steady monotone blip of the monitors; a smell of disinfectant; the squeak of nurses' white rubber soles on the polyvinyl flooring. Although bustling with energy and urgency, there is an air of confident efficiency. We go in and there, to the left, sitting up in bed is Egan, having come out from under the sedative at least one, and maybe two, days before he was expected to. He is dazed and groggy but he gives us that dazzling smile that is like a light being switched on in a dark room. His eyes are weary, his face red; he is exhausted. My heart misgives as it realises the terrible stages of recovery he now has to go through; he does not want to be here, in spite of us, in spite of Charlotte. And I know he is ashamed too, and angry at himself, for having made (what I know he'll be saying to himself) a balls-up even of this, as a character in a play by Beckett might say.

The ward is full of the bustle of doctors and nurses whose work it is to drag people back from the grim precipice where some of them, at least, want to go. They are purposeful, engaged, picking up clipboards, making notes, writing in blue large felt-tip letters on the big whiteboard above the long observation desk overlooking the row of beds, one of which Egan occupies. He has had toast and tea, he tells us. The staff are amazed he has come round so soon: a very strong metabolism, they say. The patients lie in their separate agonies and fears, and Egan, I know (because he told us later), is appalled and overwhelmed by the recollection of what he had seen while under sedation. He finds it difficult to speak to us, and it is not just because of the drugs. He had intended not ever to see us again, so this is now almost impossible to deal with; but also, amid the chemical hazes in his brain, there is imprinted the terrible image of the four horsemen he had seen at Coleraine.

It was pure fear: the fierce horsemen riding directly at him, he shrunk down in terror, seeing the great hooves of their steeds, a dark-grey turbulent agitation of noise, wind and rain. He could see the horses' flared nostrils, the corded muscles in their necks. The horsemen had staring eyes and were wielding swords. One was holding a drawn bow with an arrow in position. The image is straight out of Albrecht Dürer's visualisation of the Apocalypse, the one he cut into wood in Nuremberg in 1498 or thereabouts. Dürer was then about twenty-seven or so, Egan's age. Dürer's woodcut has entered the popular imagination and there are probably hundreds of copies of it for sale in tourist shops in Nuremberg.

As Egan's body and brain cells were reacting to the onslaught to which he had subjected them, it is not surprising that the neural pathways connected to visualisation resorted to an image embodying disaster and fear: the Dürer picture, or a version of it. The frantic electric activity in the brain, driven by chemical toxicity, will have turned to wild surges of imagining. But it is also surely the case that Egan had sight of what Dürer saw, itself related to what John of Patmos described in chapter 9 of Revelation: 'And the sixth angel sounded, and I heard a voice from the four horns of the golden altar which is before God, saying to the sixth angel which had the trumpet, Loose the four angels which are bound in the great river Euphrates. And the four angels were loosed, which were prepared for an hour, and a day, and a month, and a year, for to slay the third part of men … And thus I saw the horses in the vision, and them that sat on them, having breastplates of fire, and of jacinth, and brimstone: and the heads of the horses were as the heads of lions; and out of their mouths issued fire and smoke and brimstone.'

John of Patmos – the same person, it is said, who wrote the Gospel according to John and who was at the foot of the cross with the mother of Christ – outlines in Revelation the classic form that all imagining of the Apocalypse takes: trumpet blasts; seals being broken; angels rising out of the ancient Euphrates where they have been bound; the altar of God; utter destruction; and, at the end, the creation of a new Jerusalem, a new holy city, and the final overthrow of evil. Egan, I believe, connected into Dürer's imagery from St John's narrative, because nothing else would do to realise the kind of intuitive grasp he had of the condition in which we are in at the moment. For him, in his chemically induced trauma, the

Apocalypse was real. I am not trying to say that there is anything particularly special about this. All I'm seeking to convey is that an alert intuition will see how things are with us at any given time, and that it will tend to have recourse to the classic formulations of the profound exposure to distress to which humanity is subject, as outlined by John of Patmos, and depicted by Dürer, Blake and others.

That night in the intensive care unit at Coleraine, just before his sedation, Egan had seen the end of his life. In a sense it may even be said that he did die that night, and that the aftermath, which was to last for two months, was an intermediary state between life and death. You have already gone over if you see the angels of the Euphrates.

Six weeks or so later, on the morning of 2 January 2007, Egan is sitting in our kitchen. His mother is with him. He has been sober over Christmas and on the day before Christmas Eve he got engaged to be married to Charlotte. In December, before Christmas, Angela and I were in Slovakia where I was attending a poetry conference and afterwards visiting some friends in Prešov. Its great cathedral was charged with the energy of Christmas. Angela and I spent hours walking about the town with its elegant main street, its coffee houses with hundreds of varieties of cakes; but the most heart-warming aspect of the city at that time of the year was the fact that the square in front of the cathedral and much of the central spine of the main street running up from it had been taken over by little wooden structures: sales outlets for Christmas presents, hand-crafts, tiny restaurants and hot food bars. Some of them were under tents where delicious food could be had, as well as aromatic Christmas grog made from mulled wine and many spices, which they served in plastic cups. I had quite a few of these.

We were also, I have to admit, grateful for the break from immediate responsibility for Egan. This is not to say we weren't worried about him – anxiety was a constant – but simply by being at a distance from him meant there was nothing we could do if things went wrong, so to that limited extent we felt, I have to admit, free for a few days. On the evening of our second day in Prešov, as we were standing at a booth near the cathedral, drinking mulled red wine, Angela got a call on her mobile. It was Egan to say that he wanted to get engaged to Charlotte and did we approve? Angela, ever cautious, said that it was a bit sudden. I, the ever-hopeful optimist, was delighted. Charlotte was beautiful, and she was also deeply kind. She loved him – that was so clear – and if anyone could be a spur to sobriety and focus, then it would be her. I wished them all happiness, thinking at the same time of how Egan would have loved, at this moment, to sit with me and open a bottle of wine in celebration. My heart misgave again as I thought how arid life was going to be for him if he managed to forsake alcohol.

We had a non-alcoholic Christmas, with Rachel, Richard her husband, Killian, our eldest boy, Tiernan, the youngest – and of course Charlotte, the fiancée – all round the dinner table; festive, grateful for what we hoped would be a new beginning. But again, my mind misgave. And I was not alone in this. Immediately after dinner, Angela became faint. At first she thought it was just tiredness and went off early to bed. By the next morning a ravaging flu had set in. All her bones were aching; she didn't have the energy to get out of bed. It is quite evident now that this flu, or whatever it was, was her body caving in after months (indeed years) of strain and fear; the terror that would have been with her all through Christmas that something dreadful would happen, that Egan would end up in Casualty, beaten into insensibility, as had happened the two Christmases past.

Angela and I had now been married for thirty-six years. Rachel, our eldest, was born in Cork before we left for Leeds, where I was to become a doctoral student of Derry Jeffares, the Yeats scholar, who also gave me my first decent job. Angela had worked for the *Cork Examiner* before we got married, and supported me when I was a student. When we returned to Ireland in 1984, I took up a professorship in English at Coleraine, and the following year she started as a mature student there, reading sociology and social anthropology. I have always thought that, of the two of us, she was really the more natural academic. She loved being a student. She loved learning and the idea of learning, and revelled in the order of university life. The library she found a blissful haven and the fellowship she discovered with other students gave her immense satisfaction. She graduated in 1988 and in 1989 took over as manager of the Coleraine branch of the Citizens Advice Bureau, which she built into a forceful and thriving unit with a salaried staff complement of ten and about the same number of volunteers. All the funding for this operation she has sourced herself. Angela, an O'Riordan from Cork, has become, in the twenty years of her professional life, a leading and influential presence in the public and civic life of Coleraine. She is also the mother of four children. During the worst times, and these could go on for weeks on end, she would have to spend the night with Egan in his bed as he drank to try to still the terror. Often during the day, while she would be at work, Egan would call her up and plead with her to come home and stay with him for a while. She never refused him. I have never seen her refuse any request from anyone, if it came from genuine need and it lay in her power to grant it.

Egan managed to stay sober through the days after Christmas, but broke out on New Year's Day, in the evening. Charlotte tried to persuade him to stop. He insisted that he wasn't drinking, even though, comically, she could see him necking a vodka bottle in the kitchen through the frosted glass. She eventually decided to leave him to it, frustrated by his barefaced lies, and went back to her mother's house in Portstewart where she spent the rest of New Year's Day.

That same night, at about ten o'clock, Egan arrived at our door, slightly drunk and asking if there was anything to drink. Angela let him in and said there was a half-bottle of red wine in the house but nothing else. You are welcome to it she said, but go straight to bed. He took the bottle and a glass and went quietly to the small bedroom where he slept if he was staying at our house. In this room he had lain in many drunken stupors; a room where I had cleaned off the walls the marks of fingers, grease-stained from the fried fish suppers or burgers he would gorge on to satisfy the hunger-frenzy that would often come over him after 'a feed of drink'. Angela was expecting him to ask for more alcohol, but he didn't. He stayed quietly in bed.

The following morning I went off to work before he got up (I was Dean of a large faculty of arts at the University of Ulster, with many academic and administrative responsibilities, so 2 January was a normal working day). Angela and I had our cup of tea and toast in bed that morning like any other, made by me as usual and brought up on a tray. But today was different: we now knew that the magic of the engagement with Charlotte had not worked; it was a temporary distraction from the problem. That toast and tea was a solemn repast.

Angela told me later that when Egan got up he was shaky and withdrawn. He was now taking the drug Antabuse, the alcohol-avoidance substance, which makes you very ill if you try to drink on top of it. He was therefore now coping not just with the effects of heavy drinking, but also with the surges of revulsion his body was going through as the drug carried out its prescribed function. The chemical name for this product is Disulfiram, and in combination with alcohol it produces palpitation, vomiting, dizziness, and horrific hangovers. Angela asked him if he wanted something to eat. He said he didn't and she made him a cup of coffee which he didn't drink. He said to his mother, quietly, that we should have let him go out of life back in November when he had tried, and failed, to kill himself. 'You shouldn't have had me resuscitated,' he said. He then got up and said he was going back home. 'Please don't drink today,' Angela said. He mumbled something which may have been 'I won't'.

Back in Antrim Hospital, that Sunday in November, when he saw Angela, Rachel and me in the ward, he must have been thinking that, sadly, his time was not yet up; he had some more to go through. He had yet, in the words the faithful Kent uses at the end of *King Lear*, to be stretched out on the rack of this rough world a bit longer; save that Kent pleads with those who are trying to bring Lear back from the oblivion he now craves, after the death of his beloved daughter, to leave him alone: 'Vex not his ghost', Kent says, a line to break your heart. Egan's ghost was to be vexed yet more.

Dr Kernahan rang to see how Egan was doing, even though it was his day off; he was astonished to hear that he had come round so quickly, and remarked to us that Egan was obviously very strong and healthy to have such powers of recuperation. There is a phrase in Irish to describe this quality in a person: *teacht aniar*, meaning, literally, coming from the west, or coming back from the place into which light sinks.

Egan now began to get sleepy and we went off for lunch. We found a pub that did a Sunday carvery. Strangely, we found we were famished when we lined up at the serving counter and looked at the roast beef, the mashed potatoes, gammon roasted in a mustard and honey glaze, and turkey (it was coming up to Christmas, so the seasonal food was on). The chef, slicing off great slabs of meat, tilting the gravy boat to slather the roasts generously, kept pressing more food on us, piling up our plates as high as he could. I remember him saying to us, as he handed our plates across the glass-topped counter, 'enjoy your lunch', laughing as he did so, me thinking how difficult it would be for Egan to enjoy a meal in a place like this, how it would be a torment for him. The meal would not be a meal without a drink. If he were to have one, it would open the door to misery, while not to have one would be bleak deprivation. He was to be forever cut off from the easy fellowship expressed in the smile and good wishes of the chef, of food and drink taken in company.

When we returned to the hospital we were told that Egan would be leaving intensive care and would be returned to Causeway. Hospital.

On Monday, the day after, I went to see him at Coleraine. The room he had been assigned was in semi-darkness, at his request. He was still very remote and confused, but he had a complaint. The male ward nurse had, he said, spoken harshly to him, and made a disparaging comment about Egan's addiction, to the effect that he was taking up valuable space and wasting money, when all that was wrong with him was simply that he couldn't control himself. From Egan's description, I recognised his supposed detractor as the nurse who was on duty as I had come in. I tried to persuade Egan to forget this slight, which I was well aware could easily be imagined, but Egan was having none of it. He was adamant that I go out and speak to the nurse.

It should be said that Egan was often convinced that he was being insulted and belittled by the staff in the hospitals where he was treated, and while I am sure that these disparagements were sometimes imaginary, nevertheless I am also certain that there were occasions when he was treated shabbily by those who should have known better. There are still medical people – nurses, doctors, consultants, psychiatrists even – who cannot see alcoholism as anything other than a weakness of character. And a weakness, or a perceived weakness, in someone who depends on you is enough sometimes to call forth a self-gratifying rage of accusation.

I went out to the ward desk to speak to the nurse. I told him what my son had said. It was quite evident that, in this case, the slight was imagined. This man had nothing but concern for Egan, and even offered to speak to him and apologise if he had said something that had somehow been taken up the wrong way. The nurse was as good as his word and came back into the darkened room with me and said what he had promised to say. Egan was disarmed and now, immediately, saw the nurse as a great person. It used to hurt me to the core when I saw this in Egan: immense gratitude for ordinary decency, because this was not what he expected of people.

The nurse left, saying to Egan to press the bell beside the bed at any time if he needed anything. There was a silence between us when the nurse had gone. What do you say to a son whom you love but who places no value on the life you have given him? I then thought I would try to say something I had wanted to say for a long time, but the moment was never right: he wouldn't be sober enough to take it in, or if he were not drinking it would be an embarrassment to bring it up. What I said was this: it did not matter to me or to his mother what he did for a living, what his income or status was, as long as he was content. Silence. I went on to say that I knew he was always comparing himself to his sister and brothers, and that he felt himself to be the failure of the family. I told him that often, when he was drunk, he would say exactly that. Rachel is a theatre director, and has worked for Sir Peter Hall; Killian is a consultant psychiatrist in Edinburgh and a clinical lecturer in the great medical school there; Tiernan works with young offenders in Leicester. Egan did not have a degree and was on disability benefit because of his alcoholism. The black sheep. I said he should stop comparing himself to others; with every nerve of my being, I tried to impress upon him that, to his mother and to me, all that mattered was his peace of mind. We didn't care what he did as long as he wasn't hounded by whatever demons awakened in him the craving for drink and the oblivion it induced.

Egan began to cry hopelessly. I took his hand and started to cry as well. And then I told him that I loved him.

Some months later, after he was dead, I told my friend Patricia Noone, a psychiatrist based in Claremorris, Co. Mayo, about this conversation. Her response was an interesting one: she said that it was all very well for me to think that it didn't matter what Egan did with his life as long as he was happy, but that was not what he wanted. He had a right to his own ambitions and desires, even if they were ones he stood little prospect of achieving. She was right, of course. And very possibly his tears that day were not tears brought on by my attempt at trying to lighten his burden; they were, maybe, tears of sorrow at the great gulf between my love for him and his inability to live up to his own expectations of what that love deserved. To put it simply, as Patricia did: it may not have mattered to us what Egan did in his life, but it mattered to him.

4

The Otherworld

Patricia Noone knew Egan well, having helped him at Easter 2005, one of the darkest periods. He was living with us and drinking like crazy. This will seem strange to anyone who has not lived with an alcoholic, who may think: what the hell were they playing at? Why didn't they stop him? He was living under their roof; were they all at it? As anyone who has been close to an alcoholic knows, there is no way you can stop a person drinking who does not want to stop: argument and pleading are futile. Addiction to alcohol is as intense and as disempowering a dependency as that induced by heroin or crack cocaine. Nothing will stop the drinker getting hold of what he or she craves.

The spring of 2005 was one of those phases of grease-stained fingermarks on the walls of his room after he had wolfed down vast feeds of fish in batter or hamburgers (the voracious appetite was, in part, a kind of survival mechanism – keep the body fed – but it was also a manic guzzling of produce, a riot of need: consume as much as you can, stomach, just because you can). There were panic attacks in the middle of the night, his mother sleeping with him in a double bed in the attic, trying to calm him in his sorrow and raving. On one occasion he pleaded with me to get him drink at nine o'clock before I headed off to work. There I was, going into the supermarket at 9 a.m., relieved to find the off-licence open for business, getting funny looks as I carried out the bottles of wine. Or he would ring Brian McGill, a taxi driver whom he knew and trusted, getting Brian to pick up alcohol for him from an off-licence when he couldn't stagger there himself. His stumbling walk tore the heart out of me and scared me too: he would sometimes, out of bravado or just indifference, career across a main road growling with traffic. Not that he went out much; he would stay in the house, drinking, watching TV, or playing one of his computer games. This was the time, he told us later in a sober phase, when he once stood over the lavatory bowl forcing the raw vodka down his throat as his body was at the same time trying to reject it by vomiting it back up.

Angela and I were in a constant state of tension and fear. Each day we arrived home not knowing what the night might bring. If things did not get too bad, then there would quite likely be the continuously renewed beseechings to sit and drink with him, so we could talk. I would often agree to this, and talk would take place, but it was never anything other than a repetitious monologue about the wrongs done to him by various people, and the cruelty and neglect he said he had experienced at his old school in Coleraine, seven or eight years earlier. These accusations, and the rages and despair they roused in him, had grounds. He allowed himself to be taken advantage of in business, and there were some problems with discipline in his secondary school. There was – and it still survives to some extent – a binary system of secondary education in Northern Ireland based on academic selection at eleven (the so-called eleven plus). This is a wonderful regime for those who make the grade and gain admission to the excellent Northern Irish grammar schools, but the deficiency of this system is that those who attend the secondary schools are, in spite of the best efforts of often highly committed teachers, perceived as second rate. Worse, the pupils can sometimes see themselves as less able than their counterparts in the grammar schools. The undermining of self-worth that a two-tier education system is bound to generate will be reflected in issues of discipline, morale, and motivation. These were matters that teachers and pupils had to struggle with at the school Egan attended. Furthermore, the fact that Egan's sister and brothers all gained admission to grammar school served only to increase his feeling that he was badged with failure.

His school experiences and his unfortunate business dealings became an unfocused phantasmagoria of weltering anger in drink during interminable bouts of weeping and rage with us in early 2005.

Elvis Costello's song 'God Give Me Strength' screamed silently in the back of my mind at this time. I often thought of the Lord's Prayer. The supplicant asks the Father to forgive him his trespasses in return for forgiving those who trespass against him or her. Ultimate forgiveness depends upon an exchange, a bargain, which is no easy matter because nobody finds it easy to forgive a wrong done by another to oneself. Egan's monologues were beyond the spiritual or moral point where rights and wrongs are balanced. His state of mind was no longer granted the grace of righting wrongs. This is another sadness of the drunk. He or she is outside the interanimation of energy that is the condition of all alert beings. He or she is locked in the monolith of the self and its ever-decreasing circle of awareness. It is the condition of anti-imagination, because, as the poet Coleridge (himself no stranger to the deathly self-absorptions of drugs and alcohol) argues, the imagination requires an outgoing of the seeking spirit, a participation with the divine mind as it works through the actual.

In 'Dejection: An Ode', Coleridge writes that his 'genial spirits fail', where genial has its older meaning, connected with 'genius', a kind of attendant spirit that each person has, governing his fate and his nature. When these spirits fail, Coleridge says, all engagement with things ceases; 'outward forms' become dead things, because 'passion and … life … are within'. In this poem of 1802 Coleridge goes even further, and says that 'we receive but what we give, /And in *our* life alone does Nature live'; in which he is venturing into the same moral sphere of interactivity that the Lord's Prayer has as its central concern: that without an action of the spirit towards that which is, there outside us, fully engaged, there can be no wholeness, no integrity of being. If we cannot, for whatever reason, have that in us which can allow us to go outwards towards others, the world, nature, then there is only joylessness. If we cannot rejoice in our-selves, then there is only bleakness, a dead landscape, the world conveyed so brilliantly by Beckett in his terrible fictions. Joy, Coleridge goes on to write, is 'that sweet voice ... the luminous cloud,' from which flows 'all that charms ... ear or sight,/ All melodies [are] the echoes of that voice,/ All colours [are] a suffusion from that light'.

Coleridge, only too aware of what drugs can do to the crucial 'shaping spirit of imagination', has described the dark tower in which the mind is imprisoned when it has lost the capacity to go out to involve its activity with all that is outside it, with that which is other than itself. Egan's monologues were protests, vociferations (a word favoured by Beckett's characters to describe their endless recriminations against what life has done to them) that spiralled inwards on themselves, futile arabesques of anger going nowhere. During these exchanges he would drink more and more, trying to get his auditor (mostly me) to join him in his joyless quest for the oblivion that would grant him solace for a while. He was in a kind of hell, out of the reach of his 'genial' spirit, in what Milton calls, describing the condition of Satan in *Paradise Lost,* a 'durance vile'.

One day in February 2005, on the advice of Colin Smythe – my friend of many years – I rang Patricia Noone to ask for advice. She was consultant psychiatrist at St Mary's Hospital in Castlebar, specialising in the treatment of depression, and with a particular interest in the relationship between alcoholism and that condition. Her work in this field is groundbreaking. A forceful and energetic person, who drove herself and her team, Patricia was responsible for setting up a centre for the treatment of depression and bi-polar disorders at Swinford, Co. Mayo.

Colin, publisher of my first book, became the leading publisher of Anglo-Irish literature from around the mid-1960s. He reissued all of Lady Gregory's works in a fourteen-volume Coole edition; he republished many neglected novelists and playwrights; and he started various literary studies series which did more than anything else to establish Irish literature in English as a world-recognised academic discipline. Closely involved with the literary estate of the Mayo novelist George Moore, Colin did a great deal to make that outstanding storyteller's work more widely known. I had introduced him to Patricia Noone, who, in spite of the many demands on her time, had become the driving force in the George Moore annual festival in Mayo. She and Colin got on like a house on fire, and he came to the George Moore knees-up in Mayo, staying with Patricia at her great house, 'Brookhill', outside Claremorris. His suggestion that I seek Patricia's advice about Egan was a brilliant one. Colin had known Egan since he was a child and was very fond of him.

I was not that keen on phoning her, in that I was now engaging her in her professional role, and I was uncertain about the appropriateness of such an approach. I need not have worried. She swept aside all my misgivings. Hadn't she known Egan anyway? Hadn't he and his brother Tiernan stayed with her when we were on visits? Hadn't our two boys and her children become friends? Tiernan had stayed in touch with one of her daughters: perhaps she was the one who had asked him, on a night out in the town, what he thought of Claremorris, to which he replied: 'I dunno. Which one is she?'.

Patricia told us that she would recommend Egan for admission to the centre at Swinford where he would be well looked after. I told him what had been offered. It was also the case that his medical benefits applied in the Republic, so there would be no more than minimal charges, always something about which he would get exercised. On Good Friday morning, after a drinking binge that had gone on for several days, he told his mother that he had decided he wanted to go to Mayo. The three of us, he, his mother and I, set off immediately, having checked with Patricia if it was alright to do so. Egan insisted that he be supplied with drink for the journey. He was drinking from a bottle of wine as we headed off towards Derry, the first leg of the journey south, which would take us through Strabane, south Donegal, past Yeats's grave at Drumcliff under Ben Bulben, Sligo town, Charlestown, past Knock into Claremorris, on the great central plain of Mayo.

The Gaelic poet Anthony Raftery has written evocatively about this plain and his heart-stirring song in praise of his native place, 'Killeadan', always comes to mind as I take the road to the southwest. It was with me that bright Good Friday morning as I drove through Limavady, heading for Derry. Raftery, a blind poet who flourished around 1820, was a notorious boozer but he was greatly admired for his musical skills (he was a fiddle-player and harper) and for his often bawdy and seditious songs. In one longer piece by him called 'The Story of the Bush', he is told the history of Ireland and the wrongs done to her by England as he shelters under a large shrub from the rain. One of the choice bits of lore the shrub imparts to the poet is that Henry VIII, who founded English Protestantism out of lust, was guilty of incest. However, Raftery's song about the plains of Mayo and Killeadan is one of the great expressions of the feeling for home and one's own people in a literature not short of examples of this theme.

> Now spring is coming and the days will be gaining
> After Bridget's feast day I'll lift up my sail,
> And since I took the notion I won't stop at all now
> Till I stand in the middle of County Mayo.
> It's down in Claremorris I'll be on the first night
> And in Balla below it I'll start on the booze,
> A full month I'll give to my visit to Kiltemagh,
> And that's only two miles from Ballinamore.

Later on in the song, Raftery exclaims that if he were now standing in the middle of his own people, age would fall off him and he would be a young man again.

This song tells us many things about Ireland and about Irish culture, but foremost amongst these in this instance is the sheer force of local feeling, how important it is for the Irish to be, as Blind Raftery puts it, standing in the middle of your own people, who know you and understand you. Coming a close second to that, and connected to it, is the importance of drink to the whole network of sociability and community. And then, thirdly, there is a sense of fun and comedy. The praise of Mayo is gratifying and wonderfully complimentary, but it is also exaggerated, and in a way that will delight the locals, who will appreciate the sincerity of feeling, the flattery, but also the joke. For instance, amongst the many and various types of timber to be found growing in this amazingly fertile region of Mayo are not only such species as box, holly, and beech, but also mahogany and logwood; and so healthy is it as a place to live that no one dies.

With Egan that morning we were, to some degree, travelling back into what remains of traditional Ireland, which is more than is often thought. I did not mention Raftery to Egan, sitting drunk in the back seat of the car, but I was thinking of that blind poet and of the pure generosity of Mayo people; it always comes as a shock when you realise that there are those for whom money and self-promotion are not the only motivations. There was not an instant of hesitation on Patricia's part when I asked for her advice and help; all she thought about was what could be done, and how any practical difficulties might be overcome.

We passed through Derry on the Waterside. Just outside the city, Egan asked me to stop so he could be sick. I pulled into a layby and helped him out. He stood at the back of the car, vomiting up wine and vodka from the night before, which I could smell from his bile. I looked at the soft light of the mild day, the grass freshly growing on the island between the road and the layby, the cars drifting past, the faces staring at us as my son vomited. I saw his tortured face as the sour bile burned his throat and the drool came from his mouth.

How do you describe what such a thing feels like? Just that you are terrified of what you are now in; yet this is what is ordained for you to undergo. There is no relief, other than that which comes when the throwing up stops, and you are glad of that, that he has got that much respite, and for the peace which comes on him with the poison out of his system.

But then Egan gets back into the car and starts drinking again. He unscrews a fresh bottle of wine and takes a deep swig from the neck. We drive on south-west until we get to the twin towns of Lifford/Strabane, really one town straddling the Foyle – Strabane to the north, Lifford to the south. As we cross the bridge into the Republic, I see a lone fisherman standing midstream in the Foyle, waders up to his waist, casting the fly delicately across the placid water.

It was warm, with the clammy, oppressive heat you can get on a humid spring day. Egan was hungry, one of his drink-driven cravings for food having come over him. It was lunchtime in any case. Ahead of us, just inside the Irish border, was a roadside restaurant, a cross between a truckers' cafe and a fish and chip shop. I parked in the potholed car-park, the deep holes filled with water from the recent heavy rains, the surface of the pools shining brilliantly in the sunshine.

Egan wanted to bring the bottle of wine into the restaurant, but this was one of those places that do not serve alcohol, and we talked him out of it. Before we went inside he took a ravenous slug.

We sat at the one of the formica tables in the crowded interior. The place was full of cheerful travellers tucking heartily into vast plates of fish and chips, with peas, fried onions, tea and bread and butter. A good-looking girl came to wipe down our table and to take our order. As she was taking down what we wanted, I saw her noticing Egan, who was, as ever, striking and magnetic, even now in his gaunt, unkempt state after weeks of heavy drinking. The girl smiled and chatted to us about the heat and the strange weather, looking at Egan as she did so. Even in his haze of drunken confusion, he responded to her as he always did to courtesy. I also knew what he was thinking. About a year before, in the spring of 2004, a girlfriend from Strabane called Maria, of whom Egan was very fond, had broken up with him. The mid-Ulster accent of the girl who was talking to us brought back Maria's voice. Why is it, he said, when the girl had gone off, smiling at some remark he had made, why is it that people in Strabane are so nice? And then he started to cry. He asked me for the keys to the car. He wanted another drink to ease the pain he was going through, caused by nothing more than the kindness of a young girl doing her job. This is what it is like for the drunk: cruelty and indifference are to be expected – they are often, so you tell yourself, what has you drinking; what shatters and overwhelms you is the kindness that can be encountered in ordinary interactions. That floors you. I gave Egan the keys and he went out into the baking heat. A few minutes later he came back and ate some of the food that had now been served.

We continued south through Sligo and Tubbercurry, and on to Charlestown. After Charlestown and the town of Knock, with its basilica to commemorate the apparitions there of the Blessed Virgin, St Joseph and St John the Evangelist to many people in 1879. Before you get to Knock there is a straight stretch of road that goes on for some miles. Along part of it, on the left-hand side, the fields are fenced with concrete posts and crossbars. At one point, about five or six miles out from Charlestown, I saw, behind this fence, on a gradual incline toward some hills behind which lay the town of Ballyhaunis, a fairy rath.

As is usual with these features of the Irish landscape, the rath was a circular enclosure overgrown by trees: hawthorn, blackthorn, hazel, holly, and the sally with its light-green, almost greyish leaves. The blackthorns and the sloe bushes were in flower, the tiny frail white petals showing against the dark wood.

I remarked that we were passing a fairy fort. Egan asked me to stop, saying he wanted to get some of the flowers from the fort for his mother. I told him this was not going to be easy and in any case it was bad luck to take anything from a fairy rath. Farmers who plough up these enclosures pay the price: the breaker of the taboo has a stroke, a tractor overturns and kills him, a child dies, a woman of the family contracts cancer, a girl disappears. Of course, logic tells us this is all nonsense; there are perfectly rational explanations for the bad stuff that happens, and yet … This is the early twenty-first century and yet many people in the countryside still would not disturb a fairy rath. Although many of these forts are the survivals of the dwelling places of Iron Age communities, some of them retaining such a use into the seventeenth century, they (along with Stone Age structures such as dolmens or passage-graves) became associated in the minds of the people with the fairies, or the sídh.

The sídh are the denizens of the otherworld, and the forts are the gateways to this separate realm of being. The fairies in Irish tradition are linked to a legendary tribe of people who inhabited Ireland before the arrival of a later tribe, the sons of Míleadh, or the Milesians. This earlier tribe was known as the Tuatha Dé Danann, the people of the goddess Danu. When the Milesians (who are often associated with the Celts, relative latecomers to the island) arrived, the Tuatha Dé Danann went underground to continue to live their lives in a separate but related arena of being. A great deal of Irish folklore, legend and myth has to do with the transactions that go on between this world above ground, normal, physical, recognisable daily life, and that otherworld, which is as close as the nearest hill, yet at the same time entirely different. All kinds of taboos operate in respect of this otherworld, entrance to which is through the fairy raths. This otherworld is known in Irish under various names, all indicating a place of being that has different laws of space and time to those that work in the here and now: Tír na nÓg (the land of the young), Tír fó Thoinn (the land under the wave) and so forth.

Drink is associated with the sídh. The Dagda (meaning good God: fairies are often referred to in Ireland as the good people, so as not to anger them), one of the chief deities of the Tuatha Dé, has his palace deep inside the passage-grave of Newgrange on the Boyne, where he presides over a continuously replenished vat of beer which is dispensed to those in that world. It was a common belief that those living in this upper world eventually joined that ancestral tribe of pre-Milesians in a pagan eternity. Seán Ó Tuama, my professor of Irish when I was a student at University College Cork, once said to us in class that people in the Gaeltacht were perfectly capable of believing that after death there was the judgement, then heaven or hell or purgatory as taught by the Catholic church, while at the same time also holding on to the view that somehow they were going to go into the sídh-world and be subsumed into an ancient order of life that accorded with myth and folk-belief.

The Dagda's vat awaits. Meanwhile, up here on this surface world, temporary entrance may be had to the world under wave by purchasing with the currency of this superficial realm access to the oblivion of the land of youth. Brendan Kennelly, the poet, scholar and teacher (and a recovered alcoholic), once said to me in utter seriousness that the great attraction of drink was that it gave access to the otherworld.

Egan, my drunken son, wanting to climb over that concrete fence and go to the rath in the field outside Charlestown, was following an impulse that draws the drinker towards the mysteries of the natural world, in particular the mystery of what was once human habitation gone back into nature. Because, maybe what is magical in the fairy forts is precisely that: they embody, in the landscape, the provisionality of what is human. That we, in our arrogance, are mere ephemera. Again, Ó Tuama, talking to us about the Gaelic mind: maybe, he said, it is nature, not man, that is eternal. Those raths, in their inscrutable isolation, mostly left alone over the centuries for fear of what may be unleashed if you usurp them, hint at the irrelevance of human beings. And drunks often are all too aware of the ghastly futility and pomp of human effort. That stare they have, not of anger, but of maximised doubt, comes from looking into the fuming abyss on the edge of which are perched our towers, pylons, penthouses, banks and palaces of pleasure.

I stopped the car. Egan got out, climbed the concrete fence, balanced on top of it, then promptly fell over on to the other side. He got up and staggered across the field's fresh grass towards the rath, only to find that he was cut off from it by a stream. He called me over. I got out and climbed the fence, seeing with alarm how high the fall was on the other side, before jumping down to join him. There he was, looking about to see if there was any way he could get over the wide and fast-flowing stream. I told him to forget it; he would not get across. He wanted to take off his trousers and wade over, but I managed to talk him out of it. We turned back, me helping him over the fence. He got in and took another swig, while I started the car for the final leg to Claremorris.

5

Hallo

Brookhill, Patricia and John Noone's house, is about a mile outside Claremorris on the road to Ballinrobe. Set on a hill above a meandering river thick with lilies, it is a fine, stone-built family house. As you turn through the big iron gates, on the left is the family graveyard, where are buried the house's Victorian owners; nearby is another tiny graveyard for the house pets. There is a wild bees' nest in a high steeple over the wide front door, and in summer, standing on the steps, looking down over the deep meadow in front of the house, you can hear the continuous soft roar of the bees.

John Noone is a vet, with a huge practice in this part of Mayo, where he is respected and trusted. Patricia is spontaneous, nonchalant, with a slightly otherworldy air that belies her competence and industry. She is gifted with total assurance, and I have seen her talk to ministers and senior civil servants in a manner that indicates, without the slightest affront, that she is explaining some rudimentary and obvious thing to a somewhat slow and lacklustre pupil in a schoolroom of the 1950s. Her relaxation is underpinned by a steely authority that reminds one of a Mother Superior in a cultivated order of nuns, with a suggestion too of Cardinal Richelieu.

She greets us and brings us into a large, flag-stoned kitchen. She sits Egan, who is trembling with nerves and drink, at the big black range and Pia, Patricia's housekeeper, gives him tea and a cigarette.

Patricia gets him some medication, which has almost immediate effect, and then takes him upstairs to a little bedroom near to hers. She is going to detoxify him herself in the house before taking him in to her centre at Swinford. Afterwards, when Egan is asleep (I am so grateful for this kindness that I do not know what to do or say, so thankful am I that the poor boy's mind is at rest), she tells Angela and me, in a matter-of-fact way, that he is one of the worst cases she has ever seen. At this stage she has been looking after him for no more than an hour at most.

During that night and the night after, Patricia gets up two or three times to check Egan's medication and to give him more if it is needed. He stays in that room for two days, sweating profusely: the sheets become as wet as if they had been plunged into warm water and have to be changed three times in twenty-four hours. The alcohol is leaving his system. It turns out that he was also self-medicating with all kinds of drugs, mostly benzedrines, so the toxins in his body are legion. The medication Patricia gives him is very effective and he sleeps most of the time. I realise that Egan is being treated by one of the leading specialists in this field in Ireland.

By the time I leave, on Easter Sunday (Angela is staying on to be with him when he is admitted to Swinford; I have to go to Sardinia where I am to give a talk at an academic conference), Egan, with that remarkable power of recuperation he has, is getting better. He is sitting by the range in the big kitchen, talking and smoking with Pia (another enthusiastic puffer), laughing at her gentle mockery and drinking tea and coffee by the gallon. He is eating: bacon, scrambled eggs, toast, marmalade – wolfing it all down with relish. You can see the vitality flooding back into him. When Egan was happy, as he was then, joy just poured out of him, as if it were a kind of interior radiance. Patricia Noone had unlocked again his 'genial spirit', as Coleridge has it. In this mood, he is a blessed person and disperses around him an aura of blessedness. Thinking about him now, sitting before the range in a big old dressing gown, I am convinced he was the best person I have ever encountered. And, even in the depths of drink, the miseries that preceded those happy hours in Brookhill and those that were to succeed them, his goodness never stopped its unceasing transmission. That picture of him, thin legs crossed beneath the gown, the laughing unshaven face, the blue eyes clear again, the light coming in through the big window over the scrubbed deal breakfast table, the black-leaded range burning thick blocks of wood, is burned forever into the photographic plate of memory. There are a few instances of our lives which, looked back upon, have the quality of eternity engraved into them, a sadness – what Yeats once called an 'autumnal tinge'. This was one of those: sitting there with Angela and Pia, Egan well again, a time of radiant sweetness.

I am flying to Sardinia to lecture at a seminar on Purgatory and have chosen as text Yeats's poem 'The Cold Heaven'. What I am going to do (what I did) was to read the poem and show what intensity it has, how it is all feeling. It creates in the onward drive of the writing (the poem is just two sentences) the shock of the realisation of remorse, of inconsolable sorrow at wrongs done to those one loves: 'Until I cried and trembled and rocked to and fro,/ Riddled with light.'

My reading and account of this poem were charged with my own feelings about Egan and his present state, mixing with the emotion conjured in Yeats's words. The talk had a profound impact on the audience and that was because I was using the poem – and, to some extent the occasion – to dramatise my own turbulence and grief.

Egan's entrance into this world was unusual. He was born on 31 January 1980 in Leeds Maternity Hospital. When his mother and I arrived at the hospital at around eleven thirty that night, a nightingale was singing in the coppice facing the entrance of the hospital, a stand of trees behind a brick wall. Beyond the trees were the lighted windows of The Community of the Resurrection, a small hall of residence for Anglican students at Leeds University, where I was teaching. Angela (whose waters had now broken) and I got out of our battered blue Mini and walked up the broad steps into the hospital, where she was admitted by a big Jamaican midwife. There was no question of Angela wanting me with her while she was giving birth, so, like the traditional father-in-waiting, I stayed outside in the reception area. In what was less than half an hour, the huge black woman came out, put her arms around me and lifted me bodily off the ground, laughing and telling me I had a son. It was an effortless birth, everything happened very swiftly and easily. The Jamaican midwife said I could go in and see Angela and our new-born son.

Angela, frail and radiant, was holding him, looking at him. And there then occurred something that I know will not seem possible, but his mother and I saw it and heard it. What I am about to tell did actually happen; *we did not imagine it.*

Angela held him up to me. She remarked how thick his hair was for a new baby; and indeed Egan had arrived two weeks early. It covered his scalp with a slicked-down dark growth. And his finger-nails too, she said, were long for a newly born child. He was smiling up at me. 'Say hallo to your daddy,' she said to him. And then, I swear this, he looked up at me out of those eyes of blazing blue and said, 'hallo'. Said it there in the delivery room. I asked Angela if she had heard it. Yes, she had. 'He's been here before,' she said. The baby kept on smiling at me, as if it were he who was welcoming me into his world.

Joy just poured out of Egan when he was a child. His brother Tiernan was born a little over a year after him, and while his mother would be looking after the new baby in the mornings, Egan (we called him after the great Gaelic poet Aogán Ó Rathaille) would be content to stay in his cot, standing up and holding on to the bars, singing loudly, even though his nappy would need to be changed. His instinct was always towards compliance, a natural impulse to courtesy.

Certain things happen in one's life that cut themselves into the mind, as I said when describing that moment of Egan's becoming well in front of the range in the kitchen at Brookhill. The incisions create a picture, as if in the tablet of the memory that stays with one for as long as breath lasts. Another cut or pictorial laceration I have in my brain is the scene of one of Egan's subjections, not just to me as his father (like Jesus to his parents at Nazareth), but to the system.

We were, as I have indicated, concerned about the secondary school Egan was attending when he was about fourteen or so. We were trying to get him transferred to a grammar school, in this case the Dominican Convent in Portstewart, where his older and younger brothers were students. What we didn't know, until some time later, was that the transfer had become blocked in the bureaucracy and statistical manoeuvring that a deeply hierarchical educational system such as that in Northern Ireland will create. At one point, after a series of incidents had brought home to us how unsuitable the environment at Egan's existing school was, I decided to make a new move. I went to see the headmaster of another local grammar school, the 'Inst', or the Coleraine Academical Institution; an establishment that is classified as a 'public school' in the bizarre British educational system, where public schools, such as Eton or Harrow, are the opposite of 'public' and are very exclusive institutions indeed. There are no more than a couple of hundred or so such schools in Britain and Northern Ireland, and Coleraine 'Inst' is one of them.

The headmaster at the 'Inst' agreed to interview Egan. The building was an early-twentieth-century solid affair, with good heavy double doors of pale oak. We went into the large hallway, parquet-floored, where a few boys in blazers were wandering about. No rush, no voices raised; a sense of order prevailed. We were directed upstairs to the headmaster's study. As we climbed the stairs, I got the smell of lavender floor polish. We were in the calm light of Protestant Ulster, recalling a time before the province had torn itself apart. This was a place where a sense of earned privilege would have sought to confine prejudice and hate, where inculcated discipline would allow old persuasions and beliefs to be retained through the cultivation of virtues of responsibility and degrees of tolerance. Or at least that would have been the ideal advanced with varying levels of enthusiasm by different headmasters. And alongside that ideal there would have been always the rages of sectarian and race hatred, unavoidable in the six counties of Northern Ireland, created in the 1921 partition that was meant to secure Protestant supremacy in that part of the island. The 'Inst' was one of those institutions whose purpose was to protect and maintain this privilege and to provide, for this British statelet, its professional classes and bureaucrats. This is where Egan and I had come to. It should be said that the 'Inst', like all such institutions, had an open policy of admission. Catholics were not disbarred from entry and it had, over the years, operated a liberal admissions policy, with exam performance being the determining factor with regard to entry. But its ethos was clear; and, in any case, Catholics themselves and their clergy would tend not to opt for a school such as 'Inst'.

The headmaster, spare and lean, with a long, lightly tanned face, had the competent air of the manager of a large timber-yard, used to transactions and taking decisions. He was relaxed and quietly spoken. He would interview Egan on his own, if that was all right. I took a seat outside the study and waited for about half an hour, during which time I prayed that Egan's intelligence and his readiness to submit himself to order would become apparent to this man, who was now holding my son's fate in his hands. Egan was, at this stage, suffering from anorexia, and was seeing a child psychiatrist, who was very definitely of the view that the school Egan was attending was a major contributory factor in his illness. He had now been off school for almost two months, and the psychiatrist was certain that the progress made in that time would be immediately set back were he to return to the same place. A lot depended on this interview and on the exercise of the headmaster's discretion.

I was called back in, interview over, or at least that part of it that involved just Egan. It is what happened next that has cut itself into my memory, as acid will cut into an engraver's plate in the process of intaglio, where the image to be printed is burned into the metal and the fissures filled with ink. Such scenes do not operate in the mind as recollections merely; they have a power and energy-field that emanate from the way in which the situation they recall itself becomes a focus for a drawing together of a widely dispersed cloud of feelings and intuitions to do with the person or persons involved, one's own fears and anxieties, and an even wider sense of the baffling way in which life throws its accidents at us. This is what great painting tries to do: to create a scene that encapsulates how things are with us, while at the same time remaining open to as many impulses, strivings, uncertainties as possible.

Anyway, let me come to this moment, when I truly saw Egan's goodness and love, perhaps really for the first time in my self-absorbed and thoughtless life. He is there in the headmaster's study, sitting in an armchair, leaning forward intently, elbows on his knees, his handsome face advanced towards the light coming from the window behind the head's desk. His hands are joined between his knees, in the posture of someone listening intently to an important message. His long dark hair falls over his high forehead. I notice how thin and elegant his legs are beneath his white chinos.

The headmaster tells us that he does not want to disappoint us. Egan has been frank about why he wants to leave his present school and he believes that Egan is right: the place is not suitable for him. But it would not be a good idea for him to come to this school. There would be too much ground to make up. It could easily make matters worse and could add to Egan's sense of disappointment. It could be, in fact, a dangerous move for Egan, for us.

Now Egan speaks, giving the headmaster his title. And then he says (and this is when the acid cuts into the intaglio plate) that he promises that if he is admitted, he will work hard, as hard as he can to catch up. He knows he is behind, but he vows (and that was the word that he used, 'vow') that he will not disappoint him or abuse any trust that might be placed in him. All the time leaning forward, elbows on his knees, absolute sincerity. I do not think I have seen anything braver or more honourable in my life. Or driven by such love (in this case for his mother and for me) that he is prepared to make any sacrifice to help us achieve what we want for him. All he wants is to do what will make us content, while of course what we want is just for him to be well and happy – all any parent with any sense wants for his or her child. What have I done, I find myself thinking, to deserve such a son in this world?

The headmaster now asks Egan to step outside; he talks to me, man to man as it were, saying Egan would be better off at the Dominican Convent in Portstewart. The phrase 'among his own' is unsaid, but it is there in the background nevertheless. He is keenly aware that a Catholic at 'Inst' would probably need to be there from the start of his secondary schooling in order not to have life made difficult for him. And he is right. A clear-sighted, realistic man, he was obviously moved by the sincerity of Egan's declarations, by his vow.

As we drive home, I tell Egan he has been brave, that I am proud of him. He says nothing, thinking (probably), I've failed again. If only it could have been a group of old Jews sitting listening to him, as they listened to Christ as a boy in the temple, they would have paid attention to a boy's need, as I believe Jews do. They would have listened. They would have understood a boy's love for his father, a father's helpless love for a son.

6

Israel in Egypt

Swinford is a sad little Mayo town, past its best. You reach it from
Claremorris by taking a winding road through lakeland and bog,
with abandoned stone-built houses overlooking the pools and
gorse. When you reach Swinford, the dereliction is apparent
straightaway: warehouses on the main street, three storeys high,
built from Mayo stone and roofed in slate, now lying empty, barred
windows smashed in, grass growing from the cast-iron guttering;
one-time grocers' shops now boarded up; a gaming arcade open for
the hooded and jean-wearing young men. Fifty years earlier this
place would have been humming with commercial life and trade,
the streets lined with ponies and carts. If you looked in through the
great open doors of the warehouses, you would have seen bales of
wool trussed in hemp, jute sacks stuffed with grain; bull-nosed
lorries with huge chromium grids being loaded with flour for the
bakeries in Sligo and Galway. Green buses, smelling sweetly of
petrol fumes and leather, would have their destinations displayed
in a rectangular glass case over the driver's cab, which he would
change by twirling a device with a Bakelite handle above his head,
the roller going through the various names until it reached the
right one – Ballina, Roscommon, Athlone. Nuns and priests and
brothers in religious clothing would be everywhere. And inside the
pubs the men would be roiling in drink.

Swinford now has an air of having been left behind, as if the Celtic Tiger of the 1990s has slunk past this town of empty warehouses and woebegone drapers' shops. This is where Patricia has chosen to locate her treatment centre into which Egan is admitted. The plan is that he will undergo a course of treatment, under her general supervision, for four to five weeks, after which he will move into residential accommodation in Claremorris, a place known as Tinteán (Irish for hearth).

Patricia has raised money to take over the defunct cinema in Claremorris and turn it into a community centre. The lower floor she has converted into an exhibition space for the town; the upstairs has been transformed into sheltered housing, with individual rooms for people who are seeking to come back into the community after care; or for people who, for one reason or another, need a place of transition in a world where there is very little space for those who cannot fit in. Downstairs, with a separate entrance to the side of the old cinema, was a small flat for the residential supervisor, who turned out to be Ray Leonard, someone I had come to know years before when I had first lectured at Patricia's George Moore Festival. Ray, it turned out, had himself been through a hell of a time with depression and bipolar disorder. He, when Egan eventually came out of Swinford, would be keeping an eye on him, and this gave me no end of comfort.

After about three weeks Egan phoned us to say that he was moving out of the Swinford centre – in effect, discharging himself. This was ahead of time; Patricia was away in London with her daughter, we were at home. None of the final arrangements were in place. Egan could not be persuaded to stay on and told us that, in any case, his bed had already been allocated to someone else. I rang John Noone to ask him if he would take Egan in for just one night while we got ready to come down: it was a six-hour drive at least. That would not be a problem. I rang Ray Leonard and told him what had happened. Would he be able to take Egan in the next day? Again, there was no difficulty.

I broke down with relief on the phone and thanked Ray. Again he said that I should think nothing of it: hadn't I done an awful lot for them, he said, referring to the times when I had come to Mayo to talk on Moore. At that time Ray taught English and drama at the local secondary school. I recall very well the first time Angela and I had met him at Patricia's. Over a few glasses of wine there was an intense and deep discussion about morality, belief, and divine love. Ray had a strong bony face with pale, almost colourless skin, brown eyes and a closely cropped snow-white beard. His hair was also tightly cut and a face full of animation was given a scholarly look by his big horn-rimmed glasses. He paid attention to everything you said, weighed it, then thought would enliven his face and he would, with quiet concentration, give his view.

We drove to Mayo the following day, full of misgivings. Had Egan been drinking? Well, I know now that he had and that he had almost certainly been back on the booze during his third week at Swinford. He told us later that he used to roam around the town during the day; patients were allowed to do that. He never told us that he drank while wandering around, but I now know that for some time he stayed sober. How hard that must have been for him. I often think what his torment must have been like: the grey light, almost solid in its leaden heaviness; the sad emptiness; the ancient green paint on the dilapidated shopfronts. What else was there for him but the riot of drink and its temporary oblivion?

We met Egan at Brookhill. John was out answering calls for assistance. We took Egan around to Tinteán to see Ray and to help him move into the room assigned him. It was an intensely hot day. Ray had his door open awaiting us. Walking up the side lane that led into Ray's apartment, I could see, behind the grey galvanised fence, the waste ground onto which his door and windows looked. The weeds flourished with the avid growth of spring: great penumbras of ragwort, high thistles, nettles, tangles of vetch.

When I introduced Egan and Ray, they hit it off immediately, understanding each other in minutes. Ray had by now lost much of his ebullience, that energy that drove him on; while Egan, after his time at Swinford, was quieter too. I had the sense, with them, of two gently suffering things, two shy creatures overexposed to the sun's unrelenting light.

Ray made us sandwiches of cooked ham and soft white bread. Egan ate with relish, enjoying the fellowship, as we drank the strong dark tea. After a bit of chat about doctors and how little they knew, Ray took us round to the front to show us Egan's room which was on the floor above Ray's flat. The façade still was that of the cinema, built probably in the 1950s. It had a large concrete canopy over the entrance that made a gesture towards Art Deco and some forlorn neo-classical style favoured by builders of these pleasure palaces in the mid-twentieth century. The old foyer, which would have contained the box-office and a kiosk, was now a vestibule that led to the art gallery. There was also a lift which you took to get access to the rooms upstairs.

I noticed with horror that there was a very strong smell of rot. When I asked about this, Ray told us that the builder (typical, typical, he said) who had made the conversion had skimped on the work, omitting to lay a damp proof course before pouring in the new concrete float on the ground floor on top of the old and rotted timbers beneath. This meant that the concrete was now sitting on what was, in effect, bog. We were, Ray pointed out, no more than a couple of hundred yards from Clare Lake down the street, and the floor of the cinema was on a level with the surface of the water below, and that was when there had not been heavy rainfall. Egan seemed indifferent to the smell, which got worse as we walked along the narrow corridor to his room.

The room was tiny, with a single bed and a large stain on the grey carpet. There was a chest of drawers, an electric socket, and that was it. People have lived in places a lot worse than this but, nonetheless, this was bad. Across the corridor was the kitchen and sitting room with no external light at all lightening its putrid shadow. We moved stuff in: a TV; a CD player; clothes; coffee; toiletries; a DVD player bought in the supermarket across the road. All the while there was Egan's heartbreaking gratitude, his longing not to be any trouble to us. Each time Angela and I carried items from the car to the room, then from the lift down that rank coffin of a corridor, I got the terrible fetor rising from the bog beneath. My heart once again misgave: I knew this was not going to work. I looked out of Egan's window at the waste ground opposite. The broiling heat was still intense and you could almost see the weeds growing in the lush and sodden warmth.

Soon after, we departed to drive back to Coleraine, and we left him there bravely facing his solitude and craving, with his TV and the other bits and scraps we had brought up to that room. These are the kinds of places where the soul can die. There have been times when I would have wished to have taken on what Egan was suffering, but that day, in that place called Tinteán, I do not think I could have faced what he now had to try to face on his own, and without the comfort of the thing he wanted more than anything: alcohol.

Angela remained very quiet as we helped Egan move into this place. She does not speak about what cannot be helped. She knew, as well as I did, that the likelihood was that this new departure would end in sorrow, but she wanted to allow herself room for hope. At some stage, Egan, if he was to survive, had to make a start into a life of his own. Maybe Tinteán, dismal and sad though it was, was the place where hope could build its nest? Such were the thoughts we exchanged as we drove out of Claremorris into the evening light. Miracles can happen.

Earlier in the day, while we were eating Ray's sandwiches, our talk strayed into theology. I was telling him about a friend of mine, Joseph O'Leary from Cork, priest and a theologian, then living in Japan, and studying the relationships between Buddhism and Catholicism. For years, twenty or more, he has been on (as he puts it) a long leash from the Cork diocese, making a life for himself in Tokyo as a teacher of literature and philosophy. I was trying to explain to Ray what Joe was like and to convey the character of the man. I told Ray how I had met him.

I was about fifteen or so, sitting in the upstairs of a double-decker bus in Cork, having climbed up the metal steps holding on to the slender chromium rail. The day was wet, the windows on the upstairs were fogged up; the only other person on the top deck was a boy on one of the front seats. The bus shuddered off, lurching and swaying through the traffic, people scurrying out of its path as they crossed Patrick Street, the city's main street, with their zig-zagging rushes and halts. And then I hear this extraordinary groaning sound, halfway between a howl and a moan. It is coming from the person sitting up front. His head is going up and down, and I can see there is a rhythm to his growls and bleats. I go up to him; I recognise him as someone I had seen before on this bus, the number 3 that goes out to Ballyphehane. He is younger than me, with a huge clear brow, hair swept neatly to one side, oiled. He has large brown eyes that are now looking up at me from a book he is holding. The pages are not covered in words; it's music. He is smiling at me. 'What's that?' I ask him. 'A score,' he replies, 'of an oratorio by Handel. Wonderful thing it is, called *Israel in Egypt*. And then, to my amazement, he starts singing again – the part of Moses he tells me, loudly, now that he has an audience – in a voice that is almost entirely tuneless. 'I can't sing in tune,' he says, stopping to explain, 'but I can hear the whole thing perfectly inside my head, and I can see the desert and the tents and the Red Sea.'

This young boy went on to become a priest. We have remained friends since that day on top of the bus. There have been many memorable nights: one with him ending up standing on the counter of the Bridge Tavern on South Main Street in Cork, he in his clerical garb, declaiming my poetry to the drinkers, demanding they pay heed; another, a night in Kyoto in a small karaoke bar, Angela with us, singing songs with three or four hookers. And now, to my mind, though I'm prejudiced of course, and know nothing of the relative standing of professionals in the field, Joe O'Leary is one of the great theologians of our time.

I am telling Ray this as we eat our ham sandwiches before going upstairs to see Egan's room, and explaining some of Joe's ideas. Ray was especially interested in what Joe had to say about the Buddhist lack of concern over what we call the supernatural, the otherworld. The Buddhist focus is on the here and now, and in the inherent significance of what is the case. This appealed to Ray since he wanted to face things head on with no illusions; the same could be said of Egan. And they both found this hard to do because, to them, life revealed itself in its full totality, including its horror. They knew the terror of life to the core. This knowledge in both of them had led directly to their illnesses. On the one hand, there was in them both the unavoidable insight they were given into what life truly is, its horror and glory; on the other, there was no escape from this witness, other than drink, for Egan. But there was, Ray said, release from the continually renewing horror of actuality – love.

'Sure, Bob,' Ray said, just before we went upstairs to see the room, 'what are the miracles, only love? I mean, you can't credit that whole thing about the feeding of the five thousand and the loaves and the fishes. You can't buy into that whole supernatural thing. It would be an abomination. What happened, and I'm certain of this, Bob, is that the people there shared an experience of love so great that it felt like thousands were fed on the five loaves and the two fishes. Then you see it's all quite credible. It's not like Luke or Mark made this up. No, they are both recording something extraordinary that happened one evening near Galilee at a place called Bethsaida. There was an experience, and a real one, Bob, of shared love and illumination when reality shifted its contours so that it was as if the bread multiplied. The bread didn't change, but the reality shift was real. Love, Bob, is real.'

Egan was sitting there in the intense heat, the door open, the weeds growing wildly in the waste ground opposite; Ray, like an incarnation of Christ himself, the ordinary man charged with vision, was beside him.

*   *   *

In a few weeks everything had fallen apart. Egan would tell us later that, one day (I suspect not long after we left him there), he had wandered into the TV lounge across from his room to find, sitting in front of the TV, another resident of Tinteán, and an alcoholic. This middle-aged man had on an overcoat, in spite of the heat (it was now coming on to summer). Egan sat down and started to talk to him. The man slipped a hand into an inside pocket and produced a half-bottle of vodka. Unscrewing the cap, he took a swig, then handed the bottle to Egan. There is a desperate need in drinkers to drink together. You see this pathetic impulse towards a shared humanity whenever they congregate: laughter, bravado, tousling each other's hair, the manly swigging, head lifted up, looking to make sure the others see their brave swallows, the thoughtful wiping of the neck of the bottle before offering it on, the hearty greeting, the swaggering farewells when one or two detach themselves from the throng to head off somewhere else where the fellowship might be even better. Of course all this goes sour too in the unalterable pattern of drunkenness where bonhomie converts first to sorrow and then to rage.

Egan took the bottle and drank. In days he was buying bottles of whiskey, rum, and vodka from the off-licence across the road which I had grimly noted when he moved in. I got a call from Ray, to tell me he was bad: out of his mind, roaring in the street, out in the rain, barefoot or in his socks. The police had been around, and Egan had been taken into hospital in Castlebar, but he had demanded to be let out the following day. As soon as he was discharged, he appeared to have been set upon by two louts who robbed him of his watch, some rings, and a silver bracelet. He then ran into a supermarket where he bought vodka to calm himself down, he said, and called the police who took him back to Claremorris. That day of Ray's call or the next (I can't be sure of the chronology here, one day bled its pain into the following) we drove to Claremorris to bring Egan home.

We arrive at Tinteán to find him on the bed, in filth. We try to tidy him up a bit and eventually, after much struggle and protest, get him out to the car, Ray helping me as I half-carry Egan down the corridor and push him into the lift. He sits in the back of the car as his mother and I load his bits and pieces into the boot. Suddenly he starts roaring at us and slamming the rear window, trying to break it. He has done this once before when I was driving him home from an appointment with his GP, after he was refused the powerful sedatives he said he needed. As I was driving home that time from Portstewart, he smashed the windscreen of the car with his fist, screaming as he did so. Here he was now, trying to do it again. If he does this, I am thinking, how do I get back to Coleraine? And I realise now, in terror, that we are not just dealing with alcohol here: Egan has been taking something else, possibly diazepam, which I knew he could get off the internet from suppliers in Pakistan.

We calm him down a bit and set off, Ray standing on the pavement, looking helplessly on. We drive up the town, past the church, and head on to the new dual carriageway that will take us towards Knock and Sligo. We are no more than five or six miles from Claremorris when Egan opens the rear door and makes to throw himself out. He is play-acting now a bit and I get enraged. I slow down, and when the speed is such that he knows he is unlikely to damage himself, he throws himself out of the door I have been shouting at him to shut. In a fury of despair, I stop the car and get out, go to the side and lift him up bodily, tearing his stinking sweatshirt, and throw him back into the car. I get back in and resume the journey. This rage of mine quietens him for a bit, but he starts raving, thinking (or pretending to think) that his mother is some girl he is trying to chat up. In between times he is imploring me to stop and buy him a particular sort of burger; he keeps on saying the irritating name over and over. I tell him I will stop when I can. I am trying to get on as far as possible while there is still light. It is now about eight o'clock and as we are coming into Sligo town, darkness coming on.

Suddenly Egan hits me in the jaw from behind. He hits me hard, probably a pay-back for my rough treatment of him earlier. For the first time in my life I see stars – thousands of tiny, golden grains of light – swirling around my field of vision. We are coming up to a filling station when this happens, and, at Angela's request, I stop to give us both time to recover from the shock, and to see if I can get Egan something to eat. He gets out as I do and dislodges a jar of coffee we had put in beside him; it rolls out and smashes on the tarmac. The coffee grains scatter and glass flies. In my fear and bafflement, I try to clear up this mess, wondering what I am to do if he hits me again while I am driving at speed. What if he hits his mother, who is even more scared than I am at this savage turn of events?

In such circumstances you do not realise, at the time, how horrific they are. You just go through them. Writing now, months after I began to record these events, it is hard to believe that Angela and I got through such times, or the suicide-attempts and the death that were to follow. But you do. You go from one instant to the next in fear and trembling, but you go on. Samuel Beckett was right in *The Unnamable* when he wrote, at the end of the novel, '… you must go on, I can't go on, you must go on, I'll go on'. That puts the matter exactly. You carry on, because when you are in this world of random violence and unpredictable events, a point comes when this realm, nightmarish and all as it is, begins to have its own normality. You just go on from one thing to the next.

As I pick up the shards of glass mixed with granules of instant coffee on the garage forecourt, I think of nothing. I just experience what the moment is, having no alternative but to be there, carrying out the task the occasion has assigned me. It is, of course, nothing like the suffering that is rioting through Egan's nerves.

It is now, as I write, August 2007, and we are in our house in Donegal. It is pouring with rain outside. The fuchsia bushes are in flower, a riot of red and purple in the lashing rain. The pale green foliage, so pale as almost to become a soft grey in the heavy rain, in its subdued lack of brilliance, highlights the intense reds and purples of the bells, each inverted cup a tiny pendant universe. Before the petals of the bud open, before the anthers and filaments begin their swaying in the wind's movements, the bell is formed in such a way as to cling on to a drop of water after the rain has fallen. There are little grooves and indentations, tiny hooks, around the base of the flower-bell to create a complex holding-device to retain the precious drop of water; this is so the moisture can be sucked up through the closed petals into the ovule, the heart of the flower; this upward intake of water can now be drawn into the calyx, mix with the filtered sap, and so create a new sweetness of fresh growth. Then the flower opens itself to the air, and to all the chance it brings.

When I was small, my father showed me how you could suck the honey from the top of the fuchsia's flower-bell, the receptacle, that bit that broadens out to the globe of the inverted cup. You took a flower, put your thumbnail to the base of the cup, pushed it into the flesh to get into the nectary, not allowing it all the way through, so you could open the flower's receptacle like a flap; you then put this opened calyx to your lips and you sucked. There was a wonderful sweetness in that hanging cup, formed from the water drawn up through the stamens which mixed with the filtered juice of the tree itself, irrigated by the sap from the earth; and there was a touch of bitterness too in that nectar, from the green pith of the branches along which the sap ran to the flower heads.

When he was a boy, I in turn showed Egan how to suck the honey from the fuchsia, and he was enthralled, as he always was by the mysteries of nature. This wonder at the natural world, something innate in him, was why he became a scientist, why he wanted to know how things worked. He was as curious about plants and their biology as he was about electricity and computers. He once, in brilliant detail and with masterly exposition, explained to me the mathematical principle behind the functioning of computers. He outlined how the complexity of computer information storage, retrieval and transmission revolved around a basic opposition between zero and one. The entire infrastructure of the modern world – lighting, heat, flight paths, trains and timetables, traffic-control, money, the currency markets, trade, food, security, weather forecasts; in a word, almost all human activity that involves money and structure – was, he said, based on this opposition between nought and the first digit. That simple binary opposition was capable of limitless diversity, depending on the sequencing of the ones and the zeros and the numbers of each in their different order. This now creates the world we inhabit.

Egan delighted in the authority of numbers, because he understood that they gave him access to the codes by which our civilisation is organised. It is also the case that his understanding of the system by which most things function would make him aware of the frail vulnerability of human motive, the puny ineffectuality of much endeavour, unless the system is with you. In any case, that day he explained the binary principle to me, he was delighted with his ability to bring clarity out of complexity, making, in a haze of blue cigarette smoke, the digital signs 0/1 on a page of a school copy-book, as he illustrated the uniformity that lay behind the infinity of possibility that this simple opposition opened. To have perceived this was genius, he said, and he told me that the person who established the algebra for the basic concept was George Boole, an English mathematician, familiar to me as the first professor of mathematics at University College Cork. Egan was able to tell me something I did not know – that Boole is buried in the college grounds.

As he praised Boole's genius, I could not help thinking that there was in him something of that same quality as he explained this (to me) fairly complicated idea with such ease and clarity. Egan went on to say that this binary principle underlay almost everything, and there is much in this: the sweetness in the tiny manufactuary that is the ovule in the fuchsia receptacle, and the bitterness that rises up from the earth through the snappy green branches of the shrub; pity for the person who suffers and the fear that such may happen to us; silence and speech; life and death.

None of any of this is in my mind as I am scrabbling up the shards of broken glass on the garage forecourt outside Sligo as Egan has gone to the toilet. There is no pity, nor indeed is there much fear around in this moment of human tragedy. Aristotle said that tragedy, on the stage, purged the emotions of pity and fear, and this is true: there is a kind of relief that comes when you see depicted terrible things that can happen to men and women. At least, the tragic scene seems to imply, the human mind can show such things in some kind of form and allow us to see that they are registered in the record of our feelings, even if they are not explained, because, the tragic scene again declares, they cannot be easily unravelled. But here, on the dark forecourt, there is only the gathering up of the broken shards.

Egan comes back, saying he wants a burger. We drive through Sligo town, then on to Drumcliff where Yeats is buried in the Church of Ireland graveyard. Here we have stopped many times when Egan and Tiernan were small, to look at the grave with its dark headstone and stark and heroic message, befitting the Irish samurai-poet, 'Cast a cold eye/ On life, on death'.

Naoshige, the Japanese lord of the sixteenth century, had on his wall the following maxim: 'Matters of great concern should be treated lightly,' and it is central to samurai thinking, that death should be accepted with nonchalance. Indeed, the samurai way is the way of death. The *Hagakure* of Yamamoto Tsunetomo, written down in the early eighteenth century, says that the samurai should embrace death, which is pure knowledge; a warrior should burn all his books, since they are only delusional, and take on the way of fearlessness, which is the way of death. The treatise also says that if a man cannot achieve his aims, then he should accept death as an honourable exit from disgrace.

I think it is the case that Egan sought out death as a means of coping with his failure to achieve the goals he had set himself. But, writing this, looking out the window of our house in Donegal towards the mountains of Crocknamurrin on the right and Crocknapeast to the left, six months after Egan has died, I cannot say that I had any glimmer of heroism in my son as we drove past the grave of Ireland's samurai-poet. And, as for me, I was thinking only of getting through the hours ahead before we reached home.

7

Walking the Roads

After Sligo we come to Bundoran, 'beautiful Bundoran, by the silvery sea', as the song has it. A once-popular holiday resort, especially so in the nineteenth century when most of the grand Victorian hotels were built, it has now fallen into less-than-genteel decay. Nevertheless, it still has an appeal for day-trippers or people down for weekends from Northern Ireland; and it is also a mecca for country-music lovers. Its main street is a noisy kaleidoscope of lurid bars, slot-machine gambling joints, takeaways, souvenir emporia selling plastic leprechauns with snowy beards and knowing smiles, DVD rental stores, 'select lounges', and many fish-and-chip shops.

Egan becomes very alert to the gaudiness, the bright lights. It is now about nine o'clock, and it's dark; the streets are full of revellers, the girls wearing mini-skirts, high heels, straw hats, tee shirts. There are many youths, drunk and staggering about, some drinking out of cans and bottles on the street. This is the kind of place you go to lose yourself for a while, and I know Egan is longing to be out there, chatting up the girls, laughing, drinking. But this carry-on is not for him any more. If he starts now, he cannot stop. He asks again for a burger. I have kept on telling him that we have yet to get to a fast-food restaurant (which is true) but I now say we'll stop as soon as I can so he can get something to eat.

I wait until I get to the upper part of the town, which leads out to the road to Ballyshannon, where it is quieter, and pull in about fifty yards up the street from a chip shop. I get out to buy the food, leaving Egan and Angela in the car. As I am placing the order, I see Egan tearing past the door in a hurtling stagger. I rush out, but cannot see him. He's gone in somewhere. There are twenty or more pubs along the two sides of the street and I start ducking in and out of them, trying to find him. No sign. I go into the off-licences and in one of them the sales assistant says, yes, there was a young fellow in here a few minutes ago a bit the worse for wear; yes, shaved head, very polite he was. I come out, look about again, but there is still no sign of him.

I collect the food at the chip shop and go back to the car where I find Egan, sitting in the back with a bottle of vodka. By the look of him, he's also had a couple of quick drinks in a pub as well. He is deeply moved and is crying, saying that this fellow in the off-licence gave him the vodka for nothing, because he had been there himself and knew what it was like.

We start off again on our way to Coleraine, Egan drinking and sloppily eating the fish and chips. Eventually he falls asleep and the remaining couple of hours pass quietly.

When we get home, we have difficulty getting Egan out of the car and into the house: he is a dead weight. We manage it, Egan still in a semi-trance. We half-carry him into my study in the front room downstairs, having decided it's best if we let him sleep there on a blanket and quilt on the floor, rather than try to push him up the stairs. And then he comes to and goes berserk.

He takes the computer keyboard off my desk, yanking it clear of its connections, and hurls it across the room at a television set. The TV falls to the floor. He is now growling and screaming, red-faced, wild-eyed. Again I am thinking: this can't just be alcohol. He is crashing into things, and turning on me. He tries to hit me, lands a feeble punch or two, and begs me to hit him. I won't and I tell him I won't. Why would I? 'Because I want you to,' he says; 'you should'. No, I cannot. There is not the slightest edge of rage in me, just deep sorrow. I restrain him easily enough. But now he starts to go for his mother as well, and roars that he'll smash up the house. I know there is an element of performance in all this but there is danger too. I cannot restrain him all night. What are we to do? We're exhausted, and we've got work tomorrow. He is weak, but he is also vicious and dangerous. Against Angela's wishes, I call the police. This was a bad move.

The police come round and, as soon as they do, Egan quietens down. They ask us do we wish to press charges (they can see the damage he has done). No, we don't. Then, as they reasonably say, there is nothing they can do. They cannot arrest him. I had thought a night in the cells would cool his heels, but that isn't possible without a charge and then he would have a criminal record, as Angela points out. She has a dread (and quite rightly so) of any of us appearing on police files. The police, two decent men, suggest we contact a doctor-on-call, who will, they say, probably sedate Egan and give him and us a night's sleep.

Confusion now sets in. The doctor does come, but he tells us we should take Egan to A & E where they may admit him to the Ross Thomson Psychiatric unit. This we do. After a two- to three-hour wait (during which he grows ever more restive), Egan is sent for assessment to the unit. A consultant psychiatrist is called in (it's now about half past two in the morning) who comes to the conclusion that he is drunk, as if we needed him to tell us that. There is, it seems, no means of making an effective diagnosis until he is sober. But when will that be? Can he not, I ask, be admitted and detoxed and then assessed for treatment? Surely, I say, his drinking is itself a symptom of some underlying cause. This is a hospital, not a detox unit I am told. 'But you've done it before' (which they had); 'why can't you do it again? He needs help.' 'Yes he does, but we cannot help him until he's sober.' If he could remain sober, I argue, he wouldn't need help, or at least not as badly as he needs it now. But it is useless.

As this dreary and predictable exchange is taking place (of course they do not want a turbulent drunk in their care; and, in any case, it is clear that the consultant is one of those medics who does not see alcoholism as an illness but as a weakness) the effects of drink have worn off a little. His craving has started up again and with it his ravening needs and impulses. He hears and understands what is going on and rage overtakes him. Suddenly he lashes out at one of the nurses and tries to kick her. He misses, but there is pandemonium. I restrain him once more (it is very easy to do) but the charge nurse is appalled as he picks up a chair and throws it. 'I'm calling the police,' she says. 'We don't have to put up with this.' They don't. The police arrive in minutes, the second time they have been called out because of Egan on the same night. They are not the same officers.

They put Egan under arrest, handcuffing him and taking him away. He goes out swearing and struggling. Wearily, in a mood that is more bleak than despair (a state of mind that has at least some residual dynamic in it, whereas we now are just worn down to silent acceptance of what is), we drive back home. It is coming up to four o'clock. The police phone. They explain that they cannot keep Egan in the station unless there is a charge brought against him. They will have to release him, they say, but they will put a restraining order on him, which will require him to stay clear of the house because of the violence attempted against his parents and their property. Where is he to go, we ask? Not their concern, they say, and it should not be yours either, given what he has done tonight. It will, they say, teach him a lesson.

Later, after all this is over (because it did pass) and Egan is sober again, he tells us that when the police discharged him, he walked the streets of Coleraine for a bit, then decided to go round to the house of someone who was father to a friend of his some years before. This man, someone of about my age, came to the door, Egan told us, saw him standing there, then quickly closed the door, apologising as he did so. I cannot say I blame him. It was half past four in the morning, he was awakened out of his sleep by a knock at the door. He opened it and realised to his horror who it was, someone known to have problems. He saw this wreck before him, who has clearly been drinking for days. Egan was bruised, gaunt, unshaven; and his face and head were covered in eczema; and he had probably been thrown out by his parents. I am sure this man thought: I want none of this, I will close the door, gently, but I must close it.

And Egan's mind as he went back down that short concrete path, turning into the elegant Victorian avenue where this man lived, what was in it? Not anger, I know that for certain; just bleak surrender and submission. Of course I am sent away, he thinks. It will always be this way for me.

After that, he walked towards the river and called at another house, again the house of parents of a friend who at the time was working in London. Here too he was asked to go, but he was told to come back in the morning. He continued to walk the streets and roads for a couple of hours after that and then at about six o'clock he rang his mother. He said he was sorry; he knew he should not be calling, but he had nowhere to go. Could he come home just to sleep for a few hours, please, then he'd leave, for ever; he would not trouble us again. He was sorry, sorry.

Of course she said yes. She let him in at the door, held him in her arms, and took him into my study where the police and doctor had talked to him a few hours before. She laid him on the floor and got a duvet from his room upstairs and a blanket or two. She wrapped these around him as he lay there exhausted by rage, emotion, self-hate. Before long, in a matter of seconds, he was fast asleep. The following morning is Angela's birthday, 7 June. It is also the day of the annual general meeting of the organisation, the Citizens Advice Bureau, for which she works. She takes some of the day off but has to attend her AGM. I go in to the university to chair the June boards of examiners. It is boring, repetitive work but it is important of course, and absorbs my attention. As on so many occasions over these past years, and in the two years that are to follow, I am grateful for work and for its routines.

I call Angela throughout the day. She tells me Egan has been sleeping a good deal of the time, but when I ring her at the day's end she is anxious. He's awakened and has been trying to get up into the loft above the garage. She is worried he may fall. Our house is one of a terrace of six, built in the late Victorian period. They are large houses, ramshackle affairs, with big gardens, and to the rear a row of what would have been stables for horses, with lofts above for storing hay and tackle and where, perhaps, a stable boy might have slept. These were converted into garages in the 1940s or thereabouts. And this is where Egan is now trying to get into, up a rickety ladder. I drive home with a heavy heart, scared of what lies ahead.

I will say something of these drives home. Often I would defer them, staying on because the job requires that I do so just to get through the vast shoals of correspondence I have to deal with and all the manifold reports and strategy documents that have to be compiled (or invented) in university 'senior' management; but also because, I am afraid, it provides me with a means of putting off what has to be faced at home, which is sometimes grim. Not the noblest of motives. The drive home takes about five minutes. During this, more often than not, a leaden mass assembles in my gut, a heft of worry and fear. I feel sorry for myself; for Angela too, of course, and for Egan, but certainly for myself. Not very uplifting, I know. If Egan is sober, there is the fear that he may have fallen off the wagon by the time I get home, Angela sparing me the bad news until I have to hear it. If he has, then there is the banal predictability of drunkenness: vociferation, sentiment, stentorious demands, accusation, pleading and his insistence on more drink, more talk. My patience gets exhausted by this continual importunacy. 'We have to talk. Why won't you listen?' And the repetitions go on and on, detail piling upon detail, all of which I've heard before, the focus getting hazier and hazier. And the grief and heartbreak of being a witness to this deterioration before your very eyes. All this being dreaded on the journey home if he's drinking. And if he's not, the unworthy annoyance that it's not going to be possible for yourself to have a drink, greatly looked forward to each night. And there would be little point in sloping off to have a quiet one in the garden: he would notice the signs. But also there was the need to show solidarity in abstinence.

When I get home, Angela tells me Egan has managed to climb up into the loft space above the garage. I climb up the ladder to take a look. He's lying on the filthy, worm-eaten floorboards. He has lost control of his bladder. His face is to one side, and I can see that his nostrils are blackened from inhaling the slate and brick dust that lies thickly on the boards. His eyes are encrusted with greenish ooze. His mouth, also black, is open, and he is snoring. There are three or four empty vodka bottles around him. He has had a stash up here, hidden away against the hour of need. I climb into the loft to see if I can get him down. He is in a deep comatose sleep and cannot be wakened. I try to lift him but realise I am not going to be able, single-handed, to carry him down the ladder, which in any case might not take our combined weight, even if I could lift him up on my shoulder. I consider asking Tommy next door to give me a hand, but even if we were to succeed in lowering him, it would take us hours, involving ropes and makeshift hammocks. No, best to call the fire brigade, who will be experts at this kind of thing.

They are along in minutes. Two great red fire engines arrive, with about fifteen persons on board, klaxons blaring, and pull up on the main road outside our terrace. All fifteen of them (there are two women on the team) run in carrying oxygen, stretchers and, yes, hammock-like affairs, along with ropes, first-aid boxes and other rescue equipment. About fifty people are now stopped on the road outside, looking in, and about six or seven have gathered out back at the garage door. It is, as luck would have it, a training night for the fire brigade, so the whole team has come out. We are providing a spectacle for the Millburn Road, on which we live. The firefighters now decide they will need an ambulance as well, so they can get round the narrow laneway to the side of the house rather than stretchering Egan all the way to the main road. The ambulance arrives with its crew and there are people everywhere in paramedical gear, huge crested helmets, big boots, high-visibility clothing, belts with axes attached. It is all very impressive, yet also slightly comical.

Five or six persons go up into the loft and, after some discussion amongst themselves, strap Egan into one of the hammock-like stretchers, arrange a kind of phalanx from above from which they lower him, hand over hand, to another waiting phalanx below, all done with tremendous gentleness. There is also, unbelievably, a great deal of Coleraine humour. They are talking away loudly to Egan, hoping perhaps to break through the stupor, along the lines of: 'Overdid the old booze a bit last night then? Ah well never mind, we'll get you sorted; don't you worry, old son. Too much of a good time was it? You'll know better next time.' I am grateful for this normality in the face of utter sadness. There is a kind of heroism in their refusal to be solemn.

Egan is carried out into the mild light of this June evening. They have put him on a stand before lifting him into the ambulance. His head is flat back on the pillowless green nylon cloth that covers the pallet. His eyes are closed, encrusted with that dried green issue. His mouth is blackened, his head roughened with white flakes of eczema. He is like Jesus taken down from the cross. It is as if, in some obscure way, he is offering this suffering for us.

Once again, we are back at the A & E unit at the Causeway Hospital, except that this time Egan is brought through straightaway. He comes round in the ward, and starts shouting, but he is put on a sedative drip which relaxes him. Finally, after many hours, at about midnight, he is admitted. It has been ceaseless turmoil for about fifty hours since I got that call from Ray to tell us that he was raving in the streets of Claremorris.

The following day, after he has sobered up a bit, Egan is finally assessed by a psychiatrist and admitted to the Ross Thomson Psychiatric Unit, to our immense relief. He is safe; he will be stabilised; he will be protected. And for a while at least (though it's not very honourable to admit this) he is not our responsibility. He is now in the system, flawed and all as it is, with its regimes, its routines, its drugs, its warmth, and the strange fellowship of the ill.

8

666 and Hope's Anchor

After a few days Egan has settled into the routine of the Ross Thomson Unit. As ever, he is making friends, his irrepressible courtesy coming through. He always makes time for people when he's sober and is full of laughter and interest in what folk are doing and thinking. When we arrive for visits, he is more often than not in the tea room, where patients can wander in and out, make tea or coffee for themselves or their visitors and chat. Egan loves this, loves being master of ceremonies, fussing over us, pointing out to us the ones who have told him their life stories. He has taken to wearing bandanas, to cover his balding head. He's been losing his hair since his teens, signs again of that alarmingly rapid metabolism, as when he was born and said 'hallo' looking at me out of those azure eyes, fists closed tight, nails already fully grown. It is as if some law in his body wants him to accelerate through experience and get what is to be done on this earth over with.

Anyway, here he is now, twenty-five years of age, serving us tea and biscuits wrapped in cellophane, presented with a flourish, as if they were gifts from some mystic realm out of which has come this genie wearing a gaudy bandana. Within days his skin has cleared, the eczema gone from his scalp. He is a bit groggy from the medication they have given him, but he is in good spirits.

Egan has become friendly with a fellow patient whom I will call Julie, a tall, striking girl with blonde curly hair and a tiny rosebud mouth. She was, Egan tells us, the Northern Ireland beauty queen when she was seventeen. I can believe it, in spite of the ravages illness has worked on her. She is worn out from anxiety, hysterical emotion and drugs. Julie suffers from what is called schizo-affective disorder, a severe form of manic depression that displays extreme mood-swings of appalling turbulence. Hospitalised for months on end, she has self-harmed and attempted suicide, and has had to be sectioned – that is, detained in hospital without her consent – because she constitutes a danger to herself and possibly to others. Julie is funny, intelligent, and witty. She is also hilariously foul-mouthed and unimpressed by doctors and the medical system on which she is so dependent. Egan delights in her irreverence and daring. She and he have become too close too fast. It is now as it always is, as if he cannot abide the sluggishness of time and its processes, and wants to get to the core of experience as soon as he can, to see if, on this occasion (whatever occasion that may be), hope will not be disappointed.

Hope is the sign under which the young must work. If that is taken away, nothing has any point. Luckily for those who are young, in most cases hope recovers from the shelling of its dugouts by the artilleries of harsh fact. Its tiny flag continues to flutter aloft in spite of the wasted landscape all around: great mounds of exploded expectation, dark pools of murky betrayal, the barbed wire of self-hate. As you get older, hope seems to matter less. You get used to getting on in a kind of resolute bleakness. But when you are young, unless there is before you some prospect that you will achieve what your heart longs for, it is hard to go on.

We are now in a time, it appears, when the young can see, clearly, that it is not at all likely that they will achieve anything commensurate with what they hold in their hearts. This is not simply a matter of their own betterment in worldly terms (though it will include that); it also has to do with a need to be valued, to have some sense that they are regarded as unique and precious. In general, that is not now the case. Even the way we now refer to university students as customers or clients, tells a great deal about how we really do not care very much about them at all. They have become 'partners' in some kind of business contract where an educational service is delivered to a certain quality standard (which is all written down) on the payment of fees. The academic services are provided (or not) in an environment where risk is carefully managed in as efficient a manner as possible, so that students can proceed to the workplace and contribute to the economy. I am referring to the current culture of contractual partnership as it operates in universities mainly because it is the world with which I am most familiar; but this quasi legal and quasi commercial arrangement, and the cash nexus that underlies it, is everywhere apparent in the way we treat our young. They see this emptiness for what it is, but accept it as the way things are. The need to be valued is something they begin to accept as an encumbrance, so many of them just let it go, and the hope that belongs with it. Most young people get on with life, find solace in music, drugs, drink; they survive, as we are programmed to do. But others, in increasing numbers, go under.

*   *   *

It is now September 2007 and I am still writing in Egan's blue notebook. Since the beginning of this year there have been more than twenty reported suicides of young men in Northern Ireland. There will, of course, have been many more; this is the official figure, but you could double that at least. One of these was a boy found hanging in a public park a few days after the funeral of a friend who had also taken his own life. Hope had let down her flag.

It is not impossible that, ever since the murder of Guy Harper outside Kelly's in Portrush, Egan has been in a state of profound disbelief in the prospect of hope. *Spes* is the Latin for hope; the sign of hope is the anchor, because it grapples into the bottom of the sea of life.

In 1972, when I was at the age that Egan was at the time I am writing about, the time he was in the Ross Thomson and met Julie, I was given what for me then was a daunting, even a terrifying, task. I was asked by the then editor of the Jesuit periodical *Studies*, Father Peter Troddyn S.J. (what a Jesuit-sounding name, I recall thinking at the time), to do a review-essay on the reissue, by Faber & Faber, of three books by the Anglo-Welsh poet David Jones. *Studies* enjoyed then, and still does, a very high standing in the intellectual life of

Ireland. A quarterly review of 'letters, philosophy, and science', it brought a discriminating Catholic approach to these fields which was broad in scope and sought to achieve the highest standards of thought and scholarship. And here was I, being approached by them, on the suggestion of my English professor at Cork, Seán Lucy. So I was in real danger of not just letting myself down, but him as well. I worked hard at the books when they arrived, beautiful in their heavy paper, printed in the elegant fonts designed by Jones's friend Eric Gill, and with Jones's own lettering on the covers. It took me weeks to get through them: two long poems, *In Parenthesis* (1937, about Jones's experiences in the Great War), *The Anathemata* (1952, about history and religion), and *Epoch and Artist* (1959, a book of essays on art and sacrament). I learned an enormous amount from this intensive reading in Catholic thought and rigorous poetry of the highest ambition and reach. In particular, I recall the moving way Jones wrote about hope. In *The Anathemata* he asks, at one point, if hope can ever come again (this is 1952, remember, and that was the year of publication of a work long years in gestation) in a time when there is, '... on every commodity and on the souls of men/ the branded numerals: *sexcenti sexaginta sex.*' On every commodity, and even on men's souls, is to be seen now the mark of the beast: 666, the sign of the devil. What hope is there for hope now, he asks, for the splendour that underwrites all forms?: 'Spes!/ answer me!!/ How right you are – / blindfold's best!/ But, where d'you think the flukes of y'r hook'll hold/ next – from the *feel* of things?'

Best not to know about the future or the present in this time of uncertainty. Best to be blindfold now. But *spes*, hope, this needs somehow to be able to grapple into something solid, and certainly not into the 'feel of things', that hazy promotion of emotionality that drove much of western culture in the second half of the twentieth century, a luxuriant reneging on the will and on reason which we are paying the cost of now in the lives and deaths of our young. Why? Because at the heart of emotional sentiment lies a callous indifference to the reality of others' lives. Jones saw that the feel of things would just not do.

What can the 'flukes' of the young now grapple into, on what bedrock on the bottom of life's sea can the instrument of hope take hold? The twenty or more suicides of young men in Northern Ireland in eight months in 2007 came about because these individuals were without hope; they could not hook into a bedrock of security at the bottom of their sea of experience. And what would that give them, if they could hold fast? A sense that each one of them is something precious, something unique; a creature with an internal meaning, and not a 'commodity' (Jones's word) to be used, abused, abandoned, sold, drugged, disposed of.

I have written about the rapidity of Egan's metabolism, the urgency and impatience of his mind. This quality was in his make-up, announced by himself in the delivery room in Leeds, but it also became a mode of character, a way of proceeding with people and things. He loved electricity and the technology it drives. His hands would almost blur as he operated a computer. He taught himself the Java computing system over a weekend, from scratch. And with people too, he got to their cores very quickly. This approach to people and to technology had to do with what I have been saying about the need for the anchor of hope. He was restless to discover where the flukes of his best anticipations could hold fast. Was there something in others, in life, that would ground him?

And this was how it was with Julie. In the Ross Thomson, Egan ran his anchor down into the depths that opened up between them. Too fast, too fast. His mother and I were worried. We knew it was not a good idea for emotional relationships to develop in such places; they can be dangerous. We spoke to the consultant, and he agreed, but, as he said, there was little the hospital staff could do about it. They discouraged affairs and liaisons between patients, but these people were adults after all, and had to be allowed to make their own choices in such matters.

What is it that motivates a young woman like Julie to fall for an alcoholic? They know they are walking into trouble, and yet they do it; they allow their feelings to become entangled. I think, strangely enough, it may have something to do with an instinct for goodness. Women are often attracted to alcoholics, it is said, because of alcoholism in their fathers or in their families. The logic goes something like this: a girl experiences the hopelessness of seeing someone she loves destroying himself, so she returns to this situation in the way that people do, in that human behaviour is condemned to repeat itself, no matter how appalling the circumstance. Or, in a slightly less fatalistic version of this: a daughter, having come through the pain of not being able to do anything to help someone she loves, seeks an opportunity to put that right with some other man. But, what if it is the case that the daughter has seen, in the alcoholic father, something she admires, something connected with the very addiction itself, and she finds herself drawn to that quality in him, a quality that all alcoholics will have some portion of? And what would that be?

I do not want to idealise what is a terrible illness, but I believe there is something at the heart of this (and other) addictions that has to do with how we are, and how we take care of what Wordsworth called in 'Tintern Abbey' our 'moral being'. The poem was written on 13 July 1798, a summer of rebellion in Ireland when the insurrection was put down by the British with appalling ferocity, and when the French invasion ships arrived at Killala in County Mayo. We are now aware that we cannot separate reflections on such things as the moral being from public events, atrocities, the shunting forces of politics, military coercion. We know how alert Wordsworth always was to the state of Britain and the Union; we know that all major poets must have this alertness. So it is not an accident that Wordsworth, in 'Tintern Abbey', is trying to come to some formulation of what is inscribed in us of goodness that may, perhaps, be independent of the rages of power and oppression. This impulse towards our better nature is something we are prone all too easily to neglect, and Wordsworth speaks of being reminded of 'the language of my former heart' at Tintern Abbey, a language which is also, he says, the 'anchor of my purest thoughts'. Way in, deep down, there is an anchor of hope, or, to change the figure, a compass that points towards integrity. The hope for integrity is something the drunk has not entirely forsaken. This is what draws some women towards what, to logic, is disaster.

They say that Jesus loves a drunk. I first heard this phrase in Cork, but the great American singer Tom Waits has it in one of his songs, so it must be universal. The drunk turns aside from the push and shove, the jockeying, that goes on outside the bank where the money-changers and the traffickers in lies conduct their business. Most of us want to get into those hallowed vaults, and sell our souls so to do, but the drunk is not deceived; that refusal is an assertion, in a way, of Wordsworth's 'moral being'. And it may be what a girl sees in her beloved besotted father, and what draws her to a young man who is not deceived by the pushers and the shovers.

Women saw in Egan an integrity of the spirit, a refusal to renege on the actuality of life. Women responded to this, as did children. After he was dead and I was spending some of the most miserable days of my life clearing out his house, I came out of his front door one day and there on the pavement, looking at the house, were two children, a boy and a girl aged about six and seven. 'Mister,' they asked me, in their thick Coleraine accents, 'mister, where is the man who lived there, sir? Is he coming back?' Scarcely able to control my grief, I told them that no, he wasn't, that I was afraid that he had had an accident, that he had drowned in the river. They hadn't heard. They were shocked but didn't know what to say. Just asked me who I was. I told them. 'Well, mister,' the little girl said, 'he was very nice. He'd always talk to us.' 'And he'd laugh.' said the little boy, 'and give us money sometimes.' 'I know,' was all I could say.

This kindness and openness towards children was something I recall in a man I knew dimly in my childhood, a mysterious figure called Tom O'Dwyer. He was, I later found out, an illegitimate son of my maternal grandmother. My great-grandparents reared Tom as one of their own children. What happened to his father I do not know. My great-grandmother, a canny woman, looked out for him and set him up in business as one of Cork's first taxi drivers. This Tom, tall, red-faced, smiling, would turn up from time to time at his actual mother's house, my grandmother's, at 22 Congress Road in Cork, always the worse for drink, I suppose because he could not face her without it. But he exuded, in his drunkenness, an extraordinary kindness and it was clear that, though unmarried himself, he loved children. He would always give you half a crown and even if there were two or three of us grandchildren there, which was often the case, he would give us all the same amount. We are talking here of the early 1950s, when a working man's weekly wage would be no more than five or six pounds, so in today's money a half a crown, two shillings and sixpence, would be worth about ten pounds. A quiet, resigned person, he would sit just inside the kitchen door, in the semi-darkness, elbows on his knees, hands joined between, smiling as he'd look up at you. A patient man, submissive to life, respectful of it. Just like Egan.

9

Nobody's Inn

It will be evident by now that what I am at work on here is not a chronology of misery. It would be pointless, for me at any rate, to go through the sequence of events that led to Egan's death in order to try to produce a coherent arrangement out of them. This is not the story of an alcoholic who didn't make it: it is, I hope, a tribute to someone who was a good man. I want to record, as rawly as I can, the starts and shocks of terror we experienced as our son, a vulnerable person, underwent suffering, abuse, craving, sorrow. And why? To show the value of such a life, that such a life of suffering has, in spite of all appearances to the contrary, value, because its story reveals something of our 'moral being' which we are so good at overlooking, that it takes the vulnerable, amongst whom are the alcoholics, to reveal it to us. This is why Wordsworth, the author of that phrase 'our moral being', was drawn to the human derelicts we come across in his great poems: the beggars, the travellers, the marginalised, those who scratch a living doing spiritless jobs.

Egan was vulnerable, the word, incidentally, used by the police in January 2007 when he went missing, when he was at the bottom of the River Bann. A vulnerable person: a term for those at risk; who are not mentally stable, perhaps; who use drugs, who drink. He was vulnerable for years. Perhaps he had always been so, but if there was some innate emotional or mental instability, it came to a head during the time he attended the secondary school in Coleraine, after he 'failed' (as it is often put) the eleven-plus. He developed anorexia, was being physically intimidated at school and eventually received psychiatric treatment for his condition. The treatment was good, but I expect the trauma he went through left its mark. It is possible to have, as the cliché has it, the stuffing knocked out of you. And if that happens once, it tends to recur. In fact, Egan was forever getting beaten up. There is something about malicious men; they are not content to leave alone those they can see belong to a different level of moral being. They want to attack them, beat them to the ground. This is a fact.

One such beating occurred in the summer of 2004. In the spring of that year Egan had moved out from the family home to live in the house of someone I will call Janet. She was a rough and ready sort, but good-hearted, and took to Egan, as women so often did. Janet rented a house, sublet rooms to others (Egan amongst them) and provided a haven for drinkers and addicts. This I did not know at the time. Janet was in her forties, with the pale grey skin of a chain smoker, and the remote laxness of someone heavily dependent on prescription drugs. Her fungal, interior pallor, her lank unwashed hair, the eyes sunk back in dark sockets of exhausted skin, all emitted the air of having been sorely tried and wounded. Her speech was rapid and abrupt, and would often convey sharp dismay, angry contempt. She was someone who expected little from people, having had many disappointments. On the few occasions I had met her (once at Egan's insistence, in a bar where I was introduced to a Janet entourage of seedy hangers-on), I could see from the way she looked at Egan, the kindness in her eyes, that there was in her some impulse to look after him.

Shortly after he moved in with her, Janet and three others came round, at Egan's invitation, to our house. Egan was forever doing this, wanting new friends to meet us, wanting us to approve whatever new start he was making in his life.

It was a Saturday afternoon, a mild spring day. Janet had with her someone I took to be her boyfriend, a man called Peter. Egan let me know that Peter had been inside, he wasn't sure for what. Peter had swivelling, ferrety eyes, a thin pointed face like the front of an

axe and an urgently smiling mouth. He emitted an air of random
bustle and shifting attention, as his mind raced from one opportunity to the next. Quiet and fidgety, he gave off an air of danger. With
this Peter was a much younger man, Myler King, with a long scar
down the side of his white face, closely cropped hair, a ready smile,
and a deep insouciant confidence. He was small, but you knew this
was someone who could hurt you, as if he were made of barbed
steel, hard and brilliant, with tongues of the same material sticking
out from him, like naked blades. Myler spoke in a wheedling,
high-pitched voice that only seemed to emphasise by contrast his
implacable and vicious force. He sat with his back to the window in
our kitchen, he and Peter together, smiling, quite aware of the
discomfort they were causing and revelling in it. I could tell they
were thinking: well here we are in a place where we might have
some fun and where there may be money to be had. And what a fool
Egan was to bring us in here.

The fourth person was someone introduced to me as Myler's
girlfriend, Tanya. She was a pale, whey-faced creature, with lank
hair, like Janet's. She was thin and wore a short skirt over her bony
legs. She too was sitting with her back to the window, along with the
two men, on a low stool, and I remember her modestly pulling
down her skirt as her knees rode high. She wore white high heels
and her legs were covered in blue bruises. She also had a black eye. I
saw Myler grinning as he caught me looking at the dark bruise that
extended halfway down her cheek.

Egan made tea and brought in biscuits. He was dying to offer
them a drink, but I made no move to facilitate this. I did not relish
these people in my house. They were there because, aside from
Egan's wanting to introduce his new friends to us, a deal was being
firmed up about a Vauxhall Myler owned and an old Jaguar I had
passed on to Egan. This was an XJS, a rustbucket dating from 1996,
but a beauty in her day. I had bought this folly in the summer of
2000, in a frantic seizure of vanity, from a crook whose wife read my
fortune in the cards (this should have warned me) when I first
became Dean of Arts at the university. A little egotistical celebration of the self, the kind of thing for which you always have to pay
dearly. I told Egan he could have the car.

He had hoped to restore it. It was how he approached the world: there was always the possibility of renovation, in spite of the disappointments. Egan was like an alchemist of the defunct. He believed that, with effort and skill, old machines and power sources could be brought back to their original functions. Once, when he was aged about ten, we took him on a visit to friends of ours in the depths of west Donegal. We arrived on a dismal rain-soaked day. There was thick fog and darkness was coming on. We had to follow a track along the side of a marshy bog as we plodded towards our friends' cottage. The bog had been used as a dump for fridges, bedsteads, a car chassis, a washing machine, and suchlike, the kind of casual waste disposal you see defacing the Donegal landscape, but mostly what this dump contained, for some reason, were car batteries, hundreds of them, sunk into the ooze of the bog, hardly visible in the pouring rain and the fog as we toiled up the hill towards the cottage. Egan stopped, fascinated. He looked down into the ruck of dead batteries, with their black gleaming sides, their dull-grey lead terminal posts half-covered in soggy peat, then turned to me, looking up out of the tangle of curls with his clear blue eyes, his serious face, and said: 'You could rebuild these, Dad; you could make them work again.' He felt sorry for all that wasted power and somehow did not believe that it could be gone, that the energy that had circulated once through those acids, plates and terminals, could not be reconnected. And now we know he was right. It is now the case that, given the right conditions and mastery of the appropriate technology, it is possible to resurrect these relics of human ingenuity, but back in 1990 very few were thinking along these lines.

And so it was with the Jaguar. He hoped to renew it, and one of the sadnesses of my life was seeing, after his death, the Duckham oil he had bought to replace the soured stuff that had been in the V12 engine for years; the webbing to hold in the filler; the filler paste itself; a battery charger. Hope's anchor seeking to embed itself into the things of life.

Now some deal was underway, whereby Egan's Jaguar was to be traded for Myler's white Vauxhall, with some other elements in the transaction, the exact details of which were never revealed to me.

There was a tension-riddled traipse out through the garage to look at the Jag, me along with all of them – I wanted to keep an eye on them. The car's long red bonnet was lifted up and they admired the great engine. Peter kicked the wide tyres that helped to give the famous Jaguar floating ride. The deal was done, the Vauxhall left behind and the keys exchanged. The Jaguar had not been started for some time and Myler needed to get a mechanic on the case. No one came, and a few days later the Vauxhall disappeared, Egan telling me that Myler had taken his car back. This seemed all right to me because I was certain that Egan was not doing well out of the deal.

All this time Egan was still at Janet's. When he came round to the house, he would often be drunk and woozy. By now I had begun to realise he was taking other stuff as well as alcohol, prescription drugs, or worse; and I knew he was getting hold of whatever it was from Janet or one of her cronies. He was now implicated, to some degree, in the miserable underworld of Coleraine narcotics. This is a hellish world. In Cormac McCarthy's great novel of 2005, *No Country for Old Men*, the humane Sheriff Bell, a lawman in a Texas town, says, at one point, that if the devil were sitting around, trying to think of something that would bring the world to its knees and do his work for him, then what he would come up with would be narcotics. It was narcotics people whom Egan was hanging around with now, and there was no knowing what would happen.

The Vauxhall was gone, but the keys for the Jaguar had not been returned. Angela and I were not bothered, but we were worried about Egan's situation and were not happy that he was living with Janet, even though at this stage we did not know the full story about the drugs and the network of corruption that had ensured their supply. On the other hand, he was out of the house and there was some relief in that. It is as if he was trying to spare us having to see him forsaking his better self.

One night, Egan phones. He is in A & E where the police have taken him. He tells us he has been set upon by Myler and a friend of his, Lundy – a thug who has been a bouncer at Kelly's, where Guy was killed. Myler and his friend set upon Egan when he was walking down Union Street in Coleraine at about ten o'clock at night. They had dragged him up a side street and kicked and beaten him, for no reason, or so he says. Of course there is a reason, and it will have to do with drugs, but he does not say. All I know is that I am looking at my son in the hospital, bloody and battered, cuts all over his face, with damage to his stomach and legs. I have a feeling of utter confusion: what is going on? Who are these people and what are they up to? Egan escaped, he tells us, by running for his life and phoning the police. There is also some story about the Jaguar and its keys: that Myler is refusing to return them, while also keeping the Vauxhall.

After this assault, Egan leaves Janet's shebeen and comes back to live with us. And then there follows a baffling series of incidents: phone calls in the middle of the night with no one speaking when you pick up the receiver; possible break-ins; money disappearing; keys mislaid or lost. One day I bring home from the supermarket a six-pack carrier of wine, which I put in the pantry out of full view in order not to put temptation Egan's way: we had yet to reach the stage where we stopped drinking in the house altogether when he was around. It may not seem credible, but we have yet to realise (this is 2005) that Egan is an alcoholic. Nor do I believe he was, at this stage: an Indian physician at the hospital told him that while he was not an alcoholic, he was heading that way because he was, she said, self-medicating his depression and other problems with drink. In any case, the bottles I had hidden in the pantry disappear in a matter of hours. I ask Egan if he has taken them. No, he says, and is outraged at the suggestion. He tells me that Myler must have been in our house; he had seen him hanging around earlier in the day. He takes me into my study on the ground floor and shows me finger marks on the window on the outside, as if someone has pushed the window up to get in. He points out that I had left the catch of the window undone when I ran the cable into the socket earlier while cutting the hedge with an electric shears. He shows me marks around the Yale lock in the front door where the paint has been scratched by someone who, he says, has been trying to force it open. Egan is so convincing in all this that I believe him. I follow his advice and get a security camera and surveillance light installed over the front door.

Egan is now in pure terror of Myler and his cronies. He tells me they are out to get him, but he will not say what for, implying that it is a vendetta. He pleads with me to call Myler and tell him to lay off. I am not at all keen to do this, but I agree and make the call. I get through to Tanya, the girlfriend. She tells me she knows no one called Egan Welch. When I remind her that she has been in our house with Peter and Janet and Myler, she says she does not remember any such visit; she does not know who we are. Nor does she know anyone called Myler or Janet. I am dealing with a netherworld existence, where it is second nature never to admit to anything, to cover up, confuse, deny. After a number of other frustrating calls, I get through to Myler himself on the same number. He now also starts to create a cat's cradle of denial and misinformation, but he does admit that he knows of Egan, although he says he has never been near our house. What he says about Egan freezes the heart in me: 'He's not wise,' he says, 'and he's in trouble'. 'What kind of trouble?' I ask. 'Money trouble?' 'He knows,' says Myler, 'the kind of trouble he's in.'

Egan is listening to my side of the exchange while I am on the phone and is constantly interrupting, telling me to say this, ask Myler that. 'Tell him,' he says, 'you'll go round and kick the shit out of him.' I do not say this. When I ask Egan after I finish the call what all this is about, he tells me they are trying to frighten him. 'Why?'

'Just.'

His monosyllabic response as a kid when you'd ask him to explain why someone had done something that was out of character or not easily believable was 'Just.' I am completely at sea.

A few nights later I get a call from Egan. He had gone out at about six and we had not seen him since. We are worried, but we become even more worried when we hear what he has to say. The call comes from a pub called Nobody's Inn between Portrush and Portstewart, and Egan, in a state of panic, begs me to come and fetch him. He is with someone I will call Crane. I do not know what I am facing, but I go. Something is telling us that he is in great danger. Angela is terrified.

Nobody's Inn is on the opposite side of the road from the cliff path that runs between Portstewart and Portrush. If you cross the road and go on to the pathway, there are steep cliff falls to the black basalt rocks beneath. It is place where accidents can (and do) happen easily, and a place where it would be possible to make foul play look like mischance. At the pub, Egan is in an inner room, the shifty barman tells me. It is evident from his unease that he thinks I am the police or, perhaps, a visitant from the upper reaches of some rival outfit to that of Crane.

I go in. There is Egan, playing pool, wearing his jaunty pork-pie hat, exuding fellowship and good cheer. Full of bonhomie, he hails me, asking me to join them, telling me the man he is playing pool with is Crane, introducing me as his father. Crane is aged about thirty-five, heavily built and muscular, wearing a short-sleeved tee-shirt that shows off his thick and heavily tattooed arms. He has a shaved head above a round handsome face that does not smile as he looks at me. There is a silence. A group of people are standing around the snooker table, mostly girls about sixteen or seventeen, a couple of raw-looking boys of around the same age. I can see Crane is wondering what I am doing there, figuring out that I must have been called. He looks at Egan, asks if everything's OK. Crane is standing, feet apart, sizing me up, hands clasped around the snooker cue, the thick end of which is placed between his snow-white trainers. 'Yes, yes,' says Egan; 'Dad knew I was here.'

'How?'

I cut in: 'I rang him. I need to get him home; someone's coming round.'

I tell Egan to get a move on, trying to be as forceful as I can under the circumstances. 'No hurry,' says Egan, looking at Crane. He is dancing attendance on this man, even fawning on him. Egan tells me he wants to finish the game; there's a bet on between them. The thought comes into my head that he could be playing for his life. Under the laughing and joking he is, I know, shaking with terror. I am introduced to the others in the company. I am a ball of tension.

Egan is flinging himself around the snooker table, making slack, flashy shots, trying to be who he is imagining himself to be in his mind: Alex Higgins, the great Belfast snooker champion of the 1980s. Egan and I met him in a Soho bar the night a play about 'Hurricane' Higgins premiered in the West End of London, a play written by my son-in-law, Richard Dormer, and directed by Egan's sister, Rachel. It was a great night, a big success, and Egan and Higgins – two serious drinkers – got on famously, the latter admiring Egan's hat, the hat he is wearing now in Nobody's Inn.

Crane and his hangers-on clearly regard my son as a fool, and with the unerring instinct of the takers of this world, can see the weakness in him, the longing to be accepted, which makes him a victim and exploitable. Such people can, by instinct, spot a lack of self-worth in someone, realise it is possible to deepen that, making the victim more open to further laceration, so they can nose up to the weakened, soft underbelly and tear into it with their rows of specialised teeth. They are sharks who specialise in the feeding opportunities provided by those open to humiliation.

Crane's entourage are looking on at the snooker table with leering awareness of the tensions working away beneath the surface. The girls are wearing short skirts, high heels and exude the whiff of cheap perfume, the stuff that smells like those air fresheners you come across in taxis. I have the horrible feeling that these young women are available. Sitting on high stools, they cross their legs provocatively, wiggle their stilettos off their bare feet, pull their tight-fitting sweaters down to cover, temporarily, navels pierced with silver bands.

I tell Egan, loudly, making no attempt to cover up, that I want him out of here, and walk to the front bar, where the barman continues to eye me up. I do not buy a drink, not because I don't feel like one (I do), but because I am driving and, besides, I don't have much money on me. Egan staggers out and I see that he has, very quickly, become drunk, or perhaps he has taken something else. He fixes me with the wavering stare of the drunk and says that I must come back in and buy a drink for Crane. I refuse. He then launches into a complicated rigmarole: I must go in, otherwise they will think I am stuck up; this will reflect badly on him; he will be done for. When I ask him what all this means, he mutters that I do not understand how exposed he is; that Myler and others are involved, but that Myler and Crane hate each other. 'Are there different sides,' I ask, 'and if there are, where do you fit in?' He does not answer, nor have I the faintest idea what is afoot. Perhaps there are no sides or oppositions in this nether realm, or if there are they keep constantly changing. One thing is certain: Egan will always be on the wrong side when the axe falls. 'We've got to get out of here,' I say.

He pays no heed and says he is going back into the inner room to ask Crane to have a drink with us. I explain that I have no money and he gives me some, telling me that Crane had lent him twenty pounds earlier in the evening when he picked him up. 'Where did he pick you up?' I ask. It turns out that Egan was on the way to the off-licence when Crane stopped the car he was in and asked Egan to join him. He couldn't say no, he says, and when he told Crane that he had no money to speak of, Crane told him not to worry and gave him ('reached', the local dialect word, was the word he used) a twenty pound note. Which he now owes. Egan, terrified, goes back to the inner room.

I am trying to decide if I should follow him when he comes out with Crane and his small gang of lads and frowsty damsels. Egan, nervously grinning, indicates that they should sit with me, which they do, the girls looking at me knowingly. Egan signals with his eyes that I should buy a round, which I offer to do. Crane says he will take one, as do a couple of the others. I get myself a glass of wine. I need it. I come back to the table where they are sitting, Crane looking at me. I make small talk, remark what an awful night it is (it's been raining heavily) and that I want to get home. 'I'm sure you do,' says Crane, squeezing the muscles in his biceps with the hands of his crossed arms, smiling at me, watching. He is like a heavy dragonish creature on a ledge on a tropical island somewhere in the remotest seas under a hellish sun, watching through eyes like small metallic shutters a victim who has crawled onto the shelf of rock they now share. The tail, five feet of prehensile muscle, swishes noisily on the smooth volcanic rock, as the creature considers whether or not it will lunge now at its prey with its scaly claws, rough vicious tongue and teeth clogged with stinking carrion; or wait. This is what goes through my mind, as I think of the wet ledges of basalt across the road. Was that where Egan was to end up?

But the lunge doesn't come. We leave. I am in the car while Egan delays at the door, waving farewell to these thugs in excessive

fellowship and camaraderie. I hear from inside the mocking rau-
cous laughter and the shouts of , 'You take care now.'

On the way back in the car, Egan rambles incoherently about
Crane and his gang, about someone else called Machine and about
Myler. The network of interdependent groups is baffling. It would
be hard to know whom to trust from one day to the next and it is all
very scary. Egan is somehow mixed up in this, as is Janet. But the
leaders, the ones with the strange names, are like shoals of killer fish
shifting about and changing directions as likely prey hoves into
view. These killer shoals can turn as easily on one of their own as on
the solitary victim who unwittingly swims into range.

A few weeks later Angela accepts an invitation from our daughter Rachel and her husband Richard to join them for a week on
Crete, where they are on a fortnight's holiday. They have had a lot of
success with their stage show about 'Hurricane' Higgins and are
taking a break in a village called Sissi, which has two lovely beaches,
a still lagoon, restaurants along the seafront, and a flock of ducks
that waggle up to your dining table in the evenings. Angela needs a
break. The past six months have seen Egan grow steadily more and
more ill and, as the physician has warned, he is heading for fully
blown alcoholism. There is an increasing frequency of incidents
that involve rescue, hospitals, doctors, counsellors, appointments
broken, or, if kept, of no use because he had taken drink before
attending. The strain of coping with this has been terrible for
Angela, so when the offer comes that she should join Rachel in
Crete, I urge her to go. It will be good for her to get a break from
watching over what I am now beginning to accept may be a terminal decline.

The first day or two we are together, Egan and I get along fine.
We share a meal in the evening; there are a few drinks, but nothing
untoward. And then on the third day all hell breaks loose. I come
home in the evening from work, call out for Egan; no reply. I go
upstairs. There is a foul smell. I find him collapsed across his bed in
the small room he uses overlooking the garage at the rear of the
house. He is blind drunk and his face is covered with cuts and
bruises. He has filthied himself. I rouse him. Groaning with pain, he
tells me he has been beaten up by 'those fuckers', Myler and his
pal Lundy.

Egan starts to cry in shame and sorrow. He tells me he decided earlier in the day to get back the keys of the Jaguar. He rang Myler and he found him OK. He told Egan to come up to his house where he could collect the keys. Egan, at this stage, has a friend called Baldrick (his nickname, after Blackadder's sidekick in the BBC television series), who goes along with him. Myler answers the door and asks Egan to go round the side; he has the keys in a shed at the back of the house. Baldrick stays at the gate. When Egan goes round, Myler and Lundy set upon him. They knock him down. Egan falls against the wall and they move in, kicking and punching. They go for the stomach, ribs, and head. Egan thinks he passed out briefly, then he came to and ran for it, out to where Baldrick is standing, unaware of what had been going on. Together they make off down the hill into the town, Egan realising that he has lost control of his bowels.

I lift him off the bed where he has been lying face down as he tells me this. It is hard for him to move, but I get him into the bathroom and under the shower where I help him clean himself. I find this very difficult: there is his shame at what his body has involuntarily done; my embarrassment for him. When he is cleaned up with fresh clothes on him, I call our GP, James Harley, a kind and sorrowful man, who had lost his own son Seamus four years before.

When James examined Egan, he was shocked and furious. There were bruises all over his body, and three ribs had been cracked. He took photographs of the cuts and contusions sustained to the head and body, and insisted we report the assault to the police, who would require photographic evidence. We did call the police, who took statements and wanted us to press charges against the assailants, who were well-known to them, as long as Egan was willing to be the main witness. After a lot of thought and discussion with his mother when she got back from Crete, Egan did decide to go ahead and press charges. He was, of course, very worried. You did not cross such people lightly and he was now putting himself into danger.

The case eventually did go to trial, but not until April 2006, by which time Egan's health had seriously declined. Myler got off. His defence counsel did an excellent job deftly twisting what Egan had said to suit his own arguments. He said he believed there had never been a deal concerning a Jaguar and a Vauxhall, and that the whole situation revolved around drugs. The police had commissioned Egan to design a website for them warning young people of the dangers of drugs. Myler's defence brought this up and suggested that Egan was a reformed drug user and that was why he had done the website. He pointed out that Egan was an alcoholic (which he was by then) and had been in and out of various treatment centres (which he had between 2004 and 2006), and that he was unreliable. The judge, clearly of the view that this was a drug- and alcohol-fuelled fracas between lowlifes, threw out the case. Why should a court waste its time on these bottom-feeders of society?

10

Malocchio

In the late summer of 2004, Giuseppe Serpillo, one of my oldest friends, renewed an offer he had made a few times that we spend a few weeks at his apartment in Alghero, on the north coast of Sardinia. Giuseppe, 'Pino', is Professor of English at the University in Sassari, a city a few miles inland from Alghero. He is an embodiment of Italian courtesy and Sardinian generosity. He and his wife, Giusi, are especially fond of Egan: they love his gentleness and are impressed with the lengths he will go to please people. On a previous holiday in Alghero, Egan came with us and he loved it there. Pino and Giusi are delighted when they hear he will be with us again in the summer of 2004. They think of him like a son, is what they say.

After the assault in May, Egan has gone into a deep depression and suffers panic attacks. He drinks more than ever, using it as a way of calming his surges of terror. The flight to Sardinia is a major hurdle and he drinks to cope with it, but after a day or two, when we have settled into Pino's apartment and established a routine, he calms down. We walk through the Catalan old town to the beach, admiring the narrow cobbled streets; we hire sun loungers from a hearty, almost spherical, low-sized Sardinian. We read; I write; we swim. Or rather, Angela and I swim. The first day he is on the beach, Egan wades into the sea and cavorts around in it, but after that he stays out of the water, which is not like him at all. He has, since he was a little boy, loved swimming. He would leap about in it like a little dolphin, swimming underwater, turning head over heels, standing on his hands, then surfacing from beneath a wave, all smiles, his hair streaming. And he would be in and out of the sea for hours, just like I used to be when I was a kid. Such joy had gone out of Egan, and in his refusal to get into the water, in spite of our urgings, I realised how depressed he was.

Egan enjoyed our spherical sun-lounger attendant. We joked about the protuberance of his stomach that he advanced before him in his strutting walk, as if it were a kind of large round feeler into the variety of the life he served beneath the sun. He was glad to see us, and especially glad to see Egan, again remembering him from the last time he was there. As always, Egan was laughing, courteous, and polite, which the Sardinians recognised and respected. But over our days in the sunlight, during which we watched the holidaymakers, Sardinians and others, relaxing and taking their ease, there hung a pall of terrible sadness that made me afraid. There was a darkness in Egan that would not leave.

The attendant, also called Giuseppe, would allow us to put beer, wine and sandwiches into a fridge behind the canopy where he held court. We would eat the lunch that we had brought along with us, or I would walk up to the supermarket nearby and get pizzas freshly made, Parma ham, sweet-smelling bread. We would have a beer or wine with the food, and Egan would continue to drink through the afternoon, not much, just enough to keep the edge off. Then back about six, stopping at a café or bar overlooking the harbour for a drink or two, watching the slow, luxuriant winding down of the warm day, the gaiety, people stopping to talk across the street still astride their scooters, three or four old men sitting on a low wall chatting away, looking at the fishing boats coming and going. Life: all before us, multitudinous in its shifting interchanges, but out there, distant from Egan. In the words of Coleridge's 'Dejection: An Ode', he 'can see, not feel, how beautiful they are', the 'they' referring to the vast multiplicity of things in being. Afterwards, we go on up the Via Sassari, into the supermarket to buy the necessities, then back to the apartment. There would be more drinks before going out to eat, or Egan would cook one of his wonderful meals: chicken maybe, jointed and roasted with potatoes, lemon, onions and garlic, in olive oil and white wine. He loved the big savoury tomatoes and the garlic tinged with a blue sheen that we bought from the greengrocer up the street. He would, walking back, open the brown coarse paper bag and smell the plum tomatoes, delighting in the green aroma of the sun, leaf and plump skin. He had a capacity for total surrender to the experience of things, an impulse thwarted by his sadness. This impediment in the operation of what was his nature caused a lot of trouble for him, creating a snaggle of confused tendencies, which had a lot to do with why he drank.

There were some baffling incidents. There was, for instance, the episode with the key. Pino's apartment was entered from a lobby, a darkened hallway, which also led into another apartment exactly like ours, on the ground floor. A stairway ran from the lobby up to another floor where there was a further apartment. The lobby was entered through a shared door onto the street. To get into the apartment, you opened the street door which took you into the lobby. You then unlocked the door of the apartment itself.

One night as we were walking back from the restaurant where we had dinner, Egan said he would go on to a bar to have a late drink. We gave him the keys to the apartment after we had let ourselves in. We heard him return no more than a half an hour later as he unlocked the street door and then the inner one. Next morning, when I was going out to get some fresh bread for breakfast, I couldn't find the keys. I assumed Egan still had them, and, since he was asleep, I let him be and went out, leaving the doors ajar so I could get back in.

When I returned, he was up and about and had the coffee ready. I asked him if he had the keys; he said no, he hadn't and became irritated when I asked him to check. When he did, reluctantly, he confirmed that he did not have them. He said that when he came in he had left them where they were normally kept, on the small glass table in a long corridor that led from the door to the patio. He went to look for them there, but could not find them. This was not possible: the keys had to be in the apartment; otherwise, how could he have got in the night before? But we couldn't find them, in spite of a now panicky searching everywhere: bathroom, hallway, kitchen, kitchen-drawers, living room, dining room, the little patio where we ate. No keys. I was already in that funk you get when logic and commonsense seem to go out of the window. Egan had let himself in, therefore the keys had to be in the house. They could not be anywhere else. Against all logic (you find yourself in situations like this doing daft things because you cannot think of anything else), I went outside again to see if he had dropped the keys on the way back from the bar. That would mean that somehow he had managed to get in without them. But I had heard him unlocking the doors. Angela and I both had. I came back in and confirmed with Angela that we had heard Egan unlocking the door as he came in. All three of us searched the rooms again. Once more we could not find them. Against all logic I went back out onto the street to look around, and then, to my horror, *I saw the keys in the Yale lock to the street door.* They were not there earlier (I am absolutely certain of this) when I went out to get the bread and when I'd checked outside a few minutes before. How could they have been, when, if Egan had left them there by mistake the night before, he would have needed them to get from the outer lobby into the apartment? I came in with the keys and said to Egan that he must have found them and put them there when we were searching for them. He swore he did not do this. But he could not explain how the keys got into the lock on the outside of the street door. The only explanations possible (I went through them with him) were: (a) I had picked them up from the glass table on the way out that morning, put them in the lock, forgotten that I had done so, and failed to see them when I went outside to check if Egan had dropped them the night before; (b) when Angela and I thought the keys were lost, Egan had put them into the outside lock for some reason best known to himself.

At this time there was a bit of me that thought Egan was under some kind of hex – the evil eye, the malocchio of southern Italy and Sardinia, the piseog of Irish tradition. The evil eye, according to folklore, can come about if someone who wishes you ill gives you a certain kind of stare, which can bring misfortune to the victim if the person giving the look has the necessary power. Strange things can happen, it is believed, to those under the curse of the evil eye. The fact that I was prepared to think that there might be some nastiness afoot attributable to human agency and involving evil powers, indicates the level of stress we were under as a family. Such reactions are, I believe, not uncommon in people who are living with the realities of mental illness and addiction.

When the poet Brendan Kennelly told me that drink opens the door to the otherworld, he went on to say that it releases another set of perceptions which opens us to a separate reality. The fairy mounds in the Irish fields are symbols of that reality. The fairies, 'good people' in Irish lore, also have the power to wreak havoc in our lives if the forces they represent, that they are, are outraged or affronted by our behaviour. That is, they have the capacity to do ill and their force can be accessed by those who have the evil eye and who can, by their stare, pass the negative charge into the lives of those they hate. A piseog set on you, many Irish (and Sardinian) people believe to this day, can make strange things happen, can shift reality and make keys appear and disappear. Drink may be a door to the otherworld, but it also may be a means whereby terrible forces beyond our logic can get at us. We know this is to be the case: go to any A & E unit in a city hospital in the early hours of a Saturday morning and you will see what terrible forces drink sets free, energies that should be kept under lock and key.

That morning of the misplaced or disappearing keys, there was, I admit it, a moment of pure staring terror – that there was loose a malevolent will focused on Egan, which made ordinary logic and reality go crazy, so that material objects could start to move about subject to some remote and mischief-making will. Newton's world of gravity and mechanics, where things stayed where they were unless you moved them, seemed to be suspended, and lawless, whimsical energy seemed to have an agenda of its own jokey devising. The shock of seeing those keys in the lock of the scratched and time-worn street door, opened and closed a million times, went through me like an electric charge.

Later that morning, walking to the beach with our usual burden of towels, beachwear, books, food, we found that there was an open-air market in full swing. We wandered about in the sunshine up and down the aisles of stalls. There were outlets selling hardware, cheese, wine (farmers decanting from huge containers into two-litre plastic bottles that people brought along to be refilled), meat, rows upon rows of cured and smoked sausages, ham, whole porcettas (roast piglets) on display. With this last the butcher would lift up the whole thing and ram it into the slicer, then whang off thick slices of the cooked suckling pig, each one of which contained a green round of stuffing, breadcrumbs mixed with sage and rosemary. The smells were heavenly. The underwear stalls were an exercise in visual comedy. Monstrous bras were stretched between the metal frames that held up the coloured awnings over the counters; capacious drawers were draped across wire hangers, to the side of which tiny thongs of many colours trembled in the sea breeze. The wind had a slight touch of iodine in it; it was September, that time of year when the seaweed releases a strong and cleansing smell.

In the midst of this life and energy, evidence of how the human creature can love the experience of being alive and eating and drinking, there was the sadness of Egan, unable to be dislodged. This to him was as dust. He dragged around listlessly after us, exhausted by the effort of just being alive. I can see him still, in his shorts, his skinny legs, the gaunt handsome face with that long, slightly protruding chin, the high cheekbones, my father's cheekbones ('like Richard Widmark's', the office girls in Dunlop's Factory used to say of them, or so my father told us), the soft white cotton hat with its narrow brim that he used to cover his baldness. He looked tired and emitted a mood of utter futility, with not a trace of longing for anything, other than what is the case, with the case showing no signs of ever improving. His heavy mood was an acknowledgement that things are as they are. How it is, in that phrase of Beckett's that is the title of one of his bleakest novels, as well as being the phrase used by the bully and slavedriver Pozzo in *Waiting for Godot*. That's how it is, he says, 'on this bitch of an earth'. This is said by Pozzo, drinker and eater, owner and commander of a slave, Lucky, when he tries to express, in sentimental and sorrowful terms, the pointlessness of everything. So that, even though he has Lucky to drag around all his bits and pieces, including a chair and food to eat, and even though he can command his creature to dance and to recite for him, it is all, even for the man who appears to have control, meaningless.

Egan, a kind of Lucky, was given, by whatever mysterious law governs such things, a lot to carry about with him; he had his unfortunate 'lucky bag' to haul around, a slave to what the world had ordained for him. A lucky bag was a kind of cheap bag of sweets, costing one or two old pence, which used to be available in the Ireland of the pre-and post-war years, so they would have been known to Mr Beckett as a boy growing up in the Dublin suburb of Foxrock. You didn't ever know fully what they contained, but they would always have some sherbet and liquorice. With savage irony and, I guess, in terrible mirth, Beckett gave his Lucky a very different kind of lucky bag. Egan had his bag of troubles too, which contained the 'weight of the world'. Some people, for whatever reason, are given a lot to carry.

That morning at the market in Alghero, Egan's burden was very much in evidence, making him remote from the life that surrounded us. He was someone who wanted to be in the thick of things at the world's market, someone to whom money flowed, as it seems to flow towards certain individuals, and as it once had flowed towards him in a great spate. Ganesh Devy, an Indian friend of mine from a Brahmin family which knew about such things, once said, when Egan was a young boy, that he would make a great deal of money. And he did, for a short time. Now he had nothing – it had all been taken from him – and he was dependent on us for his needs. On that morning I saw the iron sorrow of his powerless life enter into Egan. A change came over him in the brilliant sunlight that was now, to him, just a bleak glare in the vapid and empty heat.

One afternoon in Alghero, Pino – who is something of a sooth-sayer – came, at Egan's request, to read the Tarot for him. Egan had begun to do this himself, with some success, but Pino was an expert and divination is something that Sardinians have in their blood. He and Egan retired to the apartment's rarely used dining room. On the table, covered in damask fringed with the local lacework, Pino laid out the cards which he took from the worn red bag he carried them in. It was always to be the same bag and it had to be kept in a special place in the house when not in use. I left them to it but Egan, afterwards, gave Pino permission to tell us what was revealed.

Pino, before he began, explained that the most important thing of all in a Tarot reading was the receptivity of the person telling the cards to the person for whom the reading is being done. Just as important, almost, was the willingness of the person whose fortune was being told to be open to the experience. It was, by all accounts, a very special reading. Pino told Egan what the future would hold for him, month by month, up to the end of 2005. It was going to be a difficult year, but there would be a turning point towards the end. In retrospect, Pino's forecast for the year spared nothing, but in kindness he put the most optimistic interpretation on the events as they would unfold over the next fifteen months. There were to be many treatments and hospitalisations for Egan: two in Cuan Mhuire outside Newry; two spells in Mayo, one in Swinford at Patricia Noone's place, the other in Mayo General; a period in the Ross Thomson Unit at Coleraine; four hospitalisations after A & E; and a period of treatment at St John of God's in Dublin. No wonder Pino spared both him and us. But he had seen it all, he told me after Egan died.

As well as outlining, optimistically, what the next year or so would hold for us, Pino said two other things. Our son, he told us, was an exceptionally true and simple person. That was the word he used, in its Italian form, 'simplice', carrying the full old Latin meaning of open, innocent, and sympathetic. 'There are,' Pino said, 'no secrets in him, nothing hidden, which is almost never the case. Everyone has something hidden, but not him. He is good, through and through.'

The second thing Pino had to say was that there was a possibility that there was some evil thing hanging over him, that he might be the object of someone's evil intent. He asked my permission to have his mother-in-law, Giusi's mother, carry out the old Sardinian test as to whether or not it was the case that someone had put the malocchio on him. Giusi's mother had met Egan at Pino's house in Sassari and liked him. She would be glad, Pino knew, to help if she could. Furthermore, she and a couple of friends would do this together to make the test more certain and all the stronger. Some good Sardinian witches were ready to help.

I had to provide something of Egan's to help the old ladies get a fix on him; I gave Pino one of his bandanas. The following Sunday they conducted the test. Olive oil and salt were put into water with the article of clothing near at hand. A pair of scissors was opened and closed over the water to drop the evil, if such there was, into the liquid. Iron is known universally as a charm against evil. They found that there was indeed an evil force, one of the strongest they had ever encountered. How they knew that there was was not divulged; I gather the actual method of divination must remain secret. The question now was whether or not their actions of cutting the force with the steel was effective; they would know it was if crystals were found in the water after a day or two. If crystals form, then the force had been stopped. In two days, three large crystals were found at the bottom of the glass vessel in which the test was carried out. This was a good sign and sure evidence that the malocchio had been broken. Pino brought the crystals round in a small black cylindrical capsule with a snap-on cap, the kind used to hold rolls of film. There they were, three little white rocks of salt, formed by the forces of good to stay the malocchio, after the iron in the shears had severed the power of evil.

I know this sounds strange, even a bit unhinged perhaps, but we were greatly heartened by the outcome. Egan was advised to carry the crystals with him at all times, and indeed he would take them with him when he went to Mayo for treatment in the months ahead; when he was admitted to St John of God's in Dublin; and when he moved into his house in late 2006 he put the three crystals in a little blue display frame, which he mounted on the wall of his sitting room. We have it still, and it is on the wall of the bedroom where he would, over the next two years, work through the anguishes of addiction as he fought for his life.

11

Lost to Those Waters

I started writing this memoir on 7 April 2007, less than two months after Egan drowned. It is now 4 January 2008 and we are approaching the first anniversary of his death. This writing has proceeded sporadically in the intervals of a life as a full-time academic Dean at the University of Ulster. Egan's headstone has been ordered from Cahal Newcombe of Ballycastle, Co. Antrim, one of the few remaining stonecutters in Northern Ireland. Most gravestones you see erected in graveyards these days come from China, where they are quarried and cut by computer-controlled chisels on instructions from undertakers all over the world. We have chosen Kilkenny limestone, which will be cut by Cahal himself in the old way. The lettering will be based on a font called Perpetua, devised in the 1920s by Eric Gill, the English sculptor and stonemason. It is a very simple font. The headstone will stand on the slope of St John's churchyard in Coleraine on the Derry side of the river overlooking the Bann. This grave will be mine also, and Angela's.

When Egan died, a great many people wrote letters of condolence. One of these came from the poet Seamus Heaney, the Nobel Laureate, with whom, and with his wife Marie, we have been friends for years, since 1984 in fact, when I first took up the job of heading the English department at Coleraine. But as early as 1971 he wrote to me praising a poem I had just had published in the *Irish*

Press's 'New Irish Writing' page, edited by David Marcus. The poem was based on a Gaelic original by the nineteenth-century Cork poet Mícheál Óg Ó Longáin. My poem ended with the thought that the hunger and neglect which Mícheál Óg, his wife and young family had to endure at Carrignavar, outside Cork, made 'the dead more grateful for what peace they find/ the living more cooperative with a will'. All my life I have tried to consider what the dead may teach us, and what they still may learn in their other world. Anyway, Seamus liked this piece in 1971, and took the trouble to say so.

He now wrote to say how sorry he was at our news and at the fact that he could not be at the funeral. He was recovering from a serious illness at the time and travel was out of the question. In the letter he wrote that there had always been, to his mind, something foreboding about the Bann, especially that stretch of it from Bally-money down to the Bar Mouth where it flows into the Foyle estuary. Describing it as 'unheimlich', a word meaning 'unhomely', strange, forbidding, he said that it was hard to think that Egan was 'lost to those waters'.

Heaney was right. There is something profoundly unhomely about those grey waters, as if the river herself is a kind of creature demanding offerings, sacrifice. Heaney's own work, over a long period of time, makes it clear that for him the landscape of Ireland is not simply an inert arrangement of physical matter but that it has (or we have given to it) a charge, an energy of some kind that exhibits (or we see that it exhibits) something of the continuity of a living personality; and that this entity may exact tribute. Certainly the Bann has yielded, from the Celtic period, evidence of sacrificial deposits, in particular the so-called Bann Scabbards. These are sword scabbards that were thrown into the river, into marshy land near to it, or into the groundwork for the manmade islands known as crannógs which are a feature of rivers and lakes all over Ireland. One of these scabbards, known to archaeologists as 'Bann 1', dates from about 200 BC, and was found near Toome, the site of an important ford in Celtic times. Toome is some way upriver from Coleraine, at the point where it emerges from Lough Neagh, but the scabbard is thought by some to have been manufactured near Coleraine, site of a major Bronze Age sword factory.

Water and watery places have an important place in Irish mythology. Gearóid Ó Cruadhlaoich, professor of Folklore at University College, Cork, has published a magisterial anthology of materials (as well as commentary thereon) relating to the Hag figure in Irish legend and myth. This study, called *The Book of the Cailleach*, reveals her to be a wise woman and a healer, as well as a frightening source of potential destruction if appropriate obeisance is not made to her. The stories all give the same warning: you had better be careful how you deal with the force she represents, since it is no less than the primordial energy underlying creation and which sustains the natural world, including that fraction of it that is human. She has, in Irish legend, a particular association with Beare Island in the west of present-day County Cork, but in fact she is intrinsically involved with the Irish (and indeed, Scottish) landscape as a whole and is not confined to any special region or locale.

One of the stories Ó Cruadhlaoich has collected and analysed is called 'The Hag of Beare and the Cold of May Day Monday'. Here, she is not in Cork, but on the slopes of Nephin Mountain in County Mayo, where she has been for hundreds of years, before which she lived in other places all over Ireland, in each one of which she has stayed for long periods of time: we are, as the editor points out, on the edge of primordial time and the story is about to take us right back into it. A man comes to see the Hag. He wants to know from her all about the day called May Day Monday, when thousands of years ago it became intensely cold. She, however, is not able to tell him about that Monday. Old and all as she is, something that happened as far back as that day of fierce cold is beyond what she knows, and she refers him to an creature older than she, the Eagle of the Ruined Forge. But he, like the Hag, cannot go back that far, ancient though he is, and he tells her she should go to the Otter of the Rock. He is so old that his body has worn the shape of itself into the stone on which he lies. But here too the man has no joy and the Otter says he should go, finally, to the Salmon of Assaroe on the River Erne in the north. Here at last the man finds an answer.

May Day Monday, which occurred many thousands of years ago, was, the Salmon says, so cold that when he leaped from the water to catch a fly, there came 'such thick ice on the river that it held me up when I fell back'. The Salmon, now cut off from his element, is dying in the cold when a seagull comes and pecks out one of his eyes. His own blood warms the ice and melts it so that the Salmon can get back into the water.

Here, Ó Cruadhlaoich tells us, we have a complex account of the life force 'in her destructive and nurturing powers'. The damage the seagull inflicts is what saves the salmon, a hint at the 'primal unity of the cosmic force' before it divided (or we divided it) into an opposition of positive and negative elements.

Seamus Heaney, when he wrote to me of the forbidding nature of the Lower Bann, its baleful and brooding atmosphere, was recognising the destructive power of the river, of nature herself, as figured in the Hag of Beare and the stories associated with her. Egan, as he said, was 'lost to those waters'. But Egan was also, in some other sense that we cannot fully understand, entering another world, with its own hidden reality, which only myth, cosmology, folktale and the arts of storytelling and poetry can evoke and hint at. This is a world, a continuum, where, against all logic, the destructive energies can connect with the positive ones and retrieve a unity that is primal. This interplay between what we, in our mentality of customary assumption and slack apprehension, can see only as opposition was perceived and understood as comprising some mysterious unity by the men or women who threw those beautifully worked scabbards into the grey depths of the Bann. They saw, truly saw, that life and death were implicated with each other; that life, to be a life, must include the actuality of death. The same understanding, that the destructive energies in nature are involved with its creative capacity to renew itself, lies behind the great story about the terrible cold that came in summer when the Ice Age began, and how the salmon was saved by an instinctual act of scavenging.

It is in deference to this complicated reality, as well as a testament to some form of hope (the 'spes' of David Jones) that we have asked Cathal Newcombe to carve Heaney's phrase, 'lost to those waters', into the Kilkenny limestone, which are then followed by the words of St Paul, 'risen in Christ', cut in the Perpetua font devised by Eric Gill, Jones's close friend and associate. The hope Angela and

I are trusting in here, as did Jones and Gill, is nothing less than the Christian hope of the resurrection. The mystery that is the resurrection has at its core the ancient unity of destructive and negative forces that animates not only Celtic myth, but also Greek and Roman thought, and the truth that Christianity seeks to realise. '*Et expecto resurrectionem mortuorum*': I await the resurrection of the dead, in the words of the Nicene Creed. And Dante, in Canto XIV of the *Paradiso*, expends every intellectual and emotional energy of which he is capable trying to realise this great mystery as a felt reality.

12

Head Hunters

One day in the spring of 2005, less than two years before he was drowned, Egan saw, in the Diamond, in the centre of Coleraine, some council workers felling a solitary old oak tree. It had been growing there for three or four hundred years. A few yards away were the town hall and the cenotaph commemorating the young men of Coleraine who had given their lives in two world wars. The tree now being cut down had survived the IRA bomb blast of 1992 that had ripped apart the centre of the town. It was withered and slanting over, scarcely supported by the retaining brick wall and the rusty railing around it.

When he came upon the scene, Egan, slightly drunk, was upset to see the tree being felled. By the time he arrived, the oak was being sawn into manageable segments to be carted off to the council's yard, where it would be mulched with the larger chunks being thrown into landfill sites. Offering the council workmen £20, he persuaded them to transport what remained of the trunk, a hefty cylindrical stump about five feet in length and two across, to our front garden about a quarter of a mile away. They had to use a combination of forklift and small mobile crane to get the trunk over the low wall of the flowerbed at the side of the house and to the corner of the garden where he thought it should go. In doing so, deep tracks were gouged into the lawn. With the help of the tree-fellers, Egan got the trunk standing in the corner, shaded by the branches of a lime tree.

When I got home that evening, I was shocked to see this monstrosity standing on end in the garden, four tracks cut deep into the lawn where the caterpillar plates of the crane had sunk, the raw earth exposed. When Angela told me what had happened, I started to complain about the trouble I was going to have to make good the lawn; and what was I going to do with this eyesore now sitting in our garden? 'Let it be,' she said. 'Don't give out to him. It may be his monument.' Which it did become.

Two years later, after Egan had died, I was visiting the Greater Shantallow Community Arts Centre, on the Galliagh Estate outside Derry City. I had met Oliver Green, the centre's director, at the launch of a new school of creative arts at the Magee (Derry) campus of the University of Ulster, a school I had set up, with drama, music, design, dance and digital technology being brought together for the first time. Oliver asked me to come out to Galliagh to see what they were up to and consider ways we might work together.

I met Oliver and his colleague Joe Campbell, a quiet and precisely spoken graphic novelist. They told me about the activities of the centre and gave me some background on Galliagh and the Greater Shantallow area where some 50,000 people live. The houses and flats are raw breezeblock structures that replicate themselves over bleak open spaces that were once rolling fields of farmland and pasture. About one in every twenty of the houses is burnt out. The dwellings are in widely separated clusters across which the harsh winds blow from the Foyle estuary and the flatlands leading into Inishowen in County Donegal. The green spaces are soggy beneath the grass and there is the occasional mutilated tree. It is a desolate place.

Oliver tells me that many of the people living on the estate are single mothers, in receipt of state benefit which lets them exist at subsistence level. Most families have not a single member who has ever worked. There are all the problems of places such as this: drugs, alcohol, vandalism, petty crime. The estate is provided with schools, but it is hard to get teachers to work in them. There are few other amenities. Oliver asks me if I had seen the big van parked near the centre on the way in. I had. Its four wheels were flat and I had assumed it had been abandoned or vandalised. 'No,' says Oliver. 'That's the shop.'

He shows me some of the work they have done at the centre: a CD and video of a new boy band from the estate; a newly published graphic novel about Amelia Earhart, the first woman to fly solo across the Atlantic in 1932, who landed at Culmore just outside Derry; and a recent programme on the work of the centre by network television. I am also shown photographs of tree carvings done by someone called Kieran O'Doherty. They are sculptures in oak on a very large scale, using the full width of the trunks of mature trees. The figures carved are mostly stylised faces in a Celtic style: mournful faces, long beards, the imagery influenced by popular depictions of the Celts in graphic novels or cartoons. Suddenly, it strikes me that Kieran O'Doherty may be the man to provide a solution as to what we are to do with the tree trunk Egan had moved to our garden. He had always intended getting it carved for us.

A week or so later, Kieran and I meet over a cup of tea in the refectory at Magee. It is a bright sunny day in early summer. The restaurant is closed, it being the vacation, but the chef brings us out tea and biscuits. Kieran has a sculptor's shape. He is small, stocky, dark-haired, with blunt, almost spatulate hands, the fingers all much the same length. At rest on the table, or lifting the cup of tea, his hands themselves look like powerful instruments of incision. His hair, thick and slightly greying, is swept back off his broad forehead. The face is finely cut, with a firm jawline and high cheekbones. The eyes, alert and probing, are blue-grey.

I tell Kieran about Egan, about his death, about his drink problem, about the tree stump that is a kind of monument, and I ask him if he would be interested in trying to sculpt it. He immediately grasps what I am after and declares, with an absolute and disturbing conviction, that Egan himself has chosen him to carve the tree. Kieran agrees to come round to the house and, when he does so, says again, this time to Angela also, that Egan is guiding him to the form that will emerge. He starts work in a few days, cutting away the rotten wood to get at the clean timber inside, using an axe, an adze and various hatchets. He decides to concentrate on the lower part of the trunk, where the remains of the root system are still in place, and cuts away a section of the upper half. The chunk Kieran has focused on is of a manageable size and he decides to take it over to his studio in Shantallow so he can work at it there at his ease, promising to have it in place for us when we get back from our holidays in September.

That month we spend two weeks in Crete, a holiday which brings sadness as well as relaxation. We stay in Sissi, where Angela had been when Egan was beaten up by Myler and Lundy in 2004; and Crete was the place we took Egan and Tiernan to, back in the mid-1990s, when they were thirteen and fourteen. There Egan rode a motorbike for the first time, mastering the workings of the machine in seconds, then riding up the mountainside, me behind him on the pillion seat, holding on to his ribcage, feeling the slender delicate bones beneath his white shirt billowing in the slipstream, noticing the fawn hairs on his arms stirring in the wind.

When we get back, the sculpture is in place. Kieran has inverted the trunk, so the remains of the root system are now in the air, reaching up, the branches cleaned and carved back to good timber. The object now has the appearance of something heavy and grounded flying into the air, an impression enhanced by the fact that it stands on three slender steel bars a foot or more above a base of concrete into which flat local stones have been set at angles. The whole structure has a sense of uplift, of what is weighty and massy becoming airborne, the roots searching the air, striving upwards, removed from their immersion in the cumbrous darkness of the earth. It is, in its way, a kind of resurrection, of the tree itself into sculpted form (which Egan always wanted), and of the roots, lifted out of rot and disuse and decay into hope, reaching into a new element.

There is one further thing. I notice, as Angela and I are looking at Kieran's structure striving into the light, lying nearby, a strange skull-shaped dark stone with what are, almost, the features of a stylised face on one of its facets: a nose, a thin mouth, closed eyes, all beneath a domed forehead. The whole thing looks like a head. Behind the face there is what might well be a carving of the convex shape of the skull at the back where it slopes out from the spinal cortex to create a stone version of the skull's bony globe. The small spherical dome that sits on top of a frail human neck contains all thought, writing, calculation, maps, references, mines, harbours, skyways, space, the stars, the interiors of computers, the internet, nuclear power, plutonium rods, God, love and fear of death.

Kieran, when he calls to see if we like what he has done, tells us that when, in his workshop, he cut into the lower part of the trunk where it branched out into the root system, he found, buried deep in the tangle of roots, this head-shaped stone. And he is definitely of the view that it was this embedded stone that eventually killed the tree. He can, he says, explain how the stone got in there only by suggesting that this tree grew from a sapling thrown out by a previous oak which then established a root system, as it began to flourish, around a stone placed near the original tree.

Carved stone heads feature in every manifestation of Celtic culture, a culture which, between around 300 BC to 100 AD, stretched across Europe from Ireland to Asia Minor. The poet Ovid, in exile from Rome at around the time of Christ, found himself at Tomis (now Constanza) on the Black Sea, amongst Celts, known as the Getic people. Wherever they were, the Celts gave expression to some of their deepest beliefs through a veneration for the human head.

Wooden heads have been discovered in the marshes at the source of the Seine in France: known as Sequana to the Romans, it is named after a female river deity, and her name is almost certainly cognate with that of the river Shannon. The river deity, to whom votive offerings of head-shaped objects were made, is another version of the hag figure, as in the Hag of Beare and her countless other manifestations in Irish life and culture, including Patrick Pearse's visions of her before he sacrificed himself in the Easter Rising of 1916. In a chariot grave from the fourth century BC in Waldalgesheim in Germany, a bronze curved plate was found on which is depicted a stylised head with prominent eyes. Close to it are two horns, linking the human head to the animal world; farther down are two raised arms. Raised arms, horns, and a depiction of a head: this configuration of images is very common and is to be found on the famous Gundestrup Cauldron which was found in a peat bog in Denmark in 1891. All around the outside of this cauldron are reliefs of various gods, amongst them the so-called 'horned god' or Cernunnos, which means the 'horned or peaked one'. Kieran's carving of Egan's oak stump has very clearly given it a horned or peaked appearance by shearing back the roots and inverting the whole thing, so that what were once roots are now horned peaks lifted into the air.

Cernunnos appears in euhemerised form (a technical term, meaning that an originally divine entity assumes a human identity within myth or legend) as Conall Cernach in the group of ancient Irish tales known as the Ulster Cycle. This Cycle is concerned with the exploits of the Ulaid, a powerful prehistoric people of the north of Ireland, from whom the name of the province of Ulster derives. Their enemies are the Connachta, associated with present-day Connacht, and the great conflict between them is memorialised in, amongst other tales, the famous *Táin Bó Cuailnge* (The Cattle Raid of Cooley), with its hero Cú Chulainn and the warrior queen of Connacht, Medb. Conall Cernach features in this saga and in others too. One of his boasts is that he never sleeps at night without the head of a Connachtman under his knee.

In a tale known as *The Siege of Howth*, Conall Cernach and the Ulaid defeat an invading army from Leinster at Howth outside Dublin, Conall pursuing their king Mesgedra down into Clane in present-day Kildare. There they engage in single combat. Conall kills Mesgedra, beheads him, and starts the journey back to the north in his chariot, but he has not gone very far before he encounters his victim's wife, Buan, who is returning from Meath with some women retainers. When Conall finds out who she is, he tells her that she is commanded to come with him. She asks who has given this order and he tells her that it was Mesgedra himself. Not satisfied, she demands proof that such an order has been given. He shows her her husband's horses and chariot. This will not do, she says, her husband is a man who gives many gifts. Then Conall shows her the head. Now she knows that Mesgedra is lost to her, and says so. The head blushes in Conall's uplifted hand. Conall asks Buan why it is that the head has reddened and she tells him that Mesgedra had always sworn that no Ulsterman would ever carry him away single-handed. Even in death he is ashamed at not having been as good as his word.

Conall repeats his command that she come with him as trophy, but Buan howls, falls backwards and dies. Conall leaves the head behind with her but not before he gets his charioteer to open the skull, take out the brain, mix it with lime, and squeeze it into a ball. This is now a weapon, a missile to be thrown from a sling, and it will eventually cause the death of the high king of Ulster himself.

It is evident (from this and from many other such stories) that there was a major cult of the head amongst the Celts. What I am suggesting here is that Egan unconsciously connected with those substrates of human consciousness, where stories and symbols of heads, beheadings, heads as votive offerings, cluster around realities of experience which they half-reveal, half-conceal. Egan rescues a tree trunk from a landfill by tipping a few council workers. He erects this stump in our garden as a gesture of respect towards the past. Kieran, from Derry, carves the oak, a tree that gives Derry city its name, doire being an oak grove. In Celtic legend, and in what we know of druidic belief-systems, oaks have a special significance: the druids (the word connects to the oak, 'dr' is cognate with doire) foregathered in oak groves. As he cuts into the root system of the Coleraine oak, Kieran discovers what looks like a carved head at the centre. His view is that the tree he worked on had sprung from a predecessor, at the foot of which the stone was placed, giving us a timescale for the original votive offering of as far back as 1400 or earlier, at which time pagan practices would still survive all over Ireland and Scotland. Kieran connects into the substrate of legend that has to do with heads in Celtic belief, a cult that seems to have been especially conspicuous in Ulster, evidenced in the special role assigned to the horned god Cernunnos in the figure of Conall Cernach in the Ulster stories. Kieran said many times that he was certain that he was being guided by Egan as he carved into the tree. Eventually he erects a memorial that lifts into the air. These are the roots in the midst of which he found what looks like a stone votive head. We have here a cluster of associations which, to my mind, points towards legendary significance.

Some readers may think that this is all a bit far-fetched, that these are inventions of mine on a Celtic theme, a finagling piece of distraction that is an affront to the memory of my son; what Beckett once called, in a phrase filled with a mixture of rage and shame, the 'loutishness of learning', where knowledge, or the presumption of it, is strutting inanity. But, I ask the reader to consider, is it not possible that a mind and personality as free, open, unfixed and vulnerable as my son's, can connect to strata that lie very deep in the collective mind, so deep that the normal actions of consciousness, the usual functions of reason, the usual emotions, cannot gain access to them? Indeed, it may be said that normality, so-called, is based on the very suppression of these strata in that their irruption into the ordinary affairs of life cannot be allowed because these forces and energies are, by their very nature, unpredictable and ungovernable. Otherwise, why would such institutions as the church or indeed druidism be necessary? Such institutions are, or were, required precisely because these powers need a priesthood or a magic (and their rituals) to hold them in, to harness them. And that leads to another question: where are we now with these deep energies when the old means of their ordering and formalisation, the institutions and rituals of church and magic, have lost their hold on people's minds? Have these very energies, potent, lawless, terrifying, not run riot in the craziness of drugs, money, alcohol? These powers are out, and they are out of control.

In Egan's case, it is not at all unlikely that those elements in his personality that drew him to drink also opened up access to the strata of consciousness that lie beneath the normalities of social and mental functioning. His mentality, the orientation of his character, were such that he had a feeling for ancient structures of belief and thought; such a disposition is also one that tends towards drink and the promise it holds that it enables connection with what lies deep in the mind, the contours of which overlap with Brendan Kennelly's otherworld. This combination of factors, which includes disposition, propensities, elements of weakness and openness, led Egan, through some instinctual drive, to erect in our

garden a sign that had within its cluster of meanings a dark implication from the depths of the Celtic world. An implication cut into
and opened out by the artistry of Kieran O'Doherty, a man fitted
for the work by origin, culture and temperament.

Once again, I am all too aware that the reader may be thinking,
what is he (me, that is) up to? Is he, the reader may be saying,
wanting to suggest that his son, in his drinking, was engaged in
some form of life research to gain access to Celtic roots and
archtypes? Surely, the doubting reader may think, this kind of
dallying, the pursuit of so-called original layers of culture, is
romantic delusion. And is it not dangerous also to give such credit
to what looks very like irrationality? Would it not be saner and
much more wholesome just to admit that my son was a confused
and unstable alcoholic and leave it at that?

Well, I should come straight out and say it. Yes, I do think Egan
was in search of a source, a connection between his character and
its impulses and the complicated layers of the past. This quest
(because that is what I think it was) was not done in the hope that
the outcome, were it to be attained, would resolve the problem or
give any comfort. Searches such as his are undertaken not with
these kinds of expectations; they are gone into because there is no
alternative. In our culture and our thought about that culture, there
is some sense that there are very old configurations of meaning and
emotion. It is my view that these patterns exert an allure on certain
types of personality, they pull him or her in towards them. Such a
personality – open, susceptible, enquiring – is, it may be, helpless to
withstand that dragging force, so that it becomes the means
whereby the quest into those ancient forms is undergone.

Seamus Deane, the poet, novelist, critic and scholar (and school
friend of Seamus Heaney's at St Colum's in Derry) has done more,
perhaps, than anyone else in seeking to explore the complicated
entanglements that operate in the relationships between character,
the past, tradition, nationality and addiction. His brilliant (and
brilliantly-entitled) book, *Strange Country* (1997), explores the way
in which the Irish, in the nineteenth and twentieth centuries,
thought of their condition as being a ruined and a mutilated one.
Their speech they did not reckon as a speech of any account

(I know this to be true: my own mother, God rest her, thought that the way she talked was revolting). The Irish language was, from the time of the Famine onwards, a badge of failure and disgrace. There were exceptions, of course. Cultural nationalism and the Gaelic League advanced the claims of Irish and, after the Free State was established, the language was accorded official status. However, there was a deep revulsion towards Irish, underneath the formal regard, which for years was an empty lip service confined to a few meaningless linguistic gestures, to be dispensed with as soon as possible, so that everyone could relax back into the comfort of English. But this too, this English the modernising Irish spoke, they viewed as a deformity. Hence the appalling flutings of polite Dublin English or the nasal whinings of Montenotte in Cork, grisly attempts to make sounds like those these Irish inhabitants of a linguistic nightmare imagined the posh British to emit. At heart, despising what they spoke in, estranged from the world of language their people before them had lived in, they thought of themselves as having no language to speak of.

In many nineteenth- and twentieth-century writings about the Irish they are characteristically viewed as given to excess in speech (known as 'blarney') and in drink: the 'drunken Irish'. In *Strange Country*, Seamus Deane pieces together a complex set of connections as follows: 'The sounds that issue from the mouths of the Irish – as speech, song, or wail – pose a challenge to those who wish to represent them in print. Similarly, what is taken in by those mouths – food and drink – poses a problem of another sort. Food is problematic, especially during the Famine, because there is so little of it; and drink is problematic, because there is so much of it. A starving or a drunken people obviously lack articulacy. They cannot tell their own story, nor can their story easily be told by someone else who has no experience of these extreme conditions.'

Those who do have experience of such 'extreme conditions' cannot tell their story. They are condemned to live a fate but cannot tell it. Their story has as its main theme the sense of hurt, of mutilation, they feel has been visited on them. This mutilation is not just personal; it is also historical and ancestral. It is difficult to find the words for this, but what I am suggesting is that there is a continuum of experience between historical mutilations and the failure to articulate them and the condition of certain individuals who have, by temperament or mischance, been fated to go through the consequences of those past traumas and the silence that surrounds them. History is very much alive in what we do, to ourselves and to others. Inwardly I howl with derision at those historians who pertly announce that history is about what was the case, as if the facts can be that easily posited.

The inarticulacy of those for whom the 'extreme conditions' of historical nightmare remain alive in their memories and nerves is a terrible incapacity, but that very incapacity is itself a symptom that, deep down, there is some story to be inarticulate about. They become haunted by the 'unsayability' of that which refuses to yield to language. The drunk is frequently someone who has a story to tell, one rooted in past damages and silences, many of them historical, but who cannot find the means to tell it: hence the significant groanings and banal, obsessive repetitions of drunks. They feel that there is something hidden in the root system of their being, and they know that whatever it is is connected to how they are the way they are. But the drink, which is a symptom of the problem they must suffer deep down, is that which disables them from trying to begin the vital work of disentanglement of the twisted systems of pain, anger and tortured memory within. Drink attracts because it opens awareness to the otherworld where such hurts and losses persist, form, re-form, and these the personality craves to clarify; but it is also the means whereby this clarification is frustrated. William Empson, in one of those scorching poems of his, writes of something like this contradictory torment when he says, 'and I, a twister, love what I abhor'. Egan, in the latter part of his life, would sometimes tell his mother how much he had come to hate drink and yet he could not keep away from it. It dragged him in, because it gave access to the world of feeling, deep within, where all that traumatised him lay; but it was also the very thing that prevented him from bringing that world into clarity. And I, a twister, love what I abhor.

Egan wrote, in the blue notebook in which I began this account (I have now filled it and moved on to another, a golden one this time), his suicide note of November 2006, which included the following: 'If I die it is not alcohol that killed me, it's something else?' What that something else was he did not know, and could not say. But I do think that Egan's 'something else?' was connected to the search he was engaged upon into the mutilations visited upon his character by certain extreme conditions within the Irish experience to this day. The tree he rescued from the landfill site, the sacrificial oak (if I may now call it that), was a totem of his historical and personal sorrow. And, as his mother saw, that day when I came back from work to find this lump of tree in our garden, it has now, as carved by an O'Doherty from the city of the oak itself, become a monument to his integrity of pain. Seamus Deane in one of his poems writes: 'history is personal'. It sure as hell is.

13

Creating Haddock

Egan was not simply a 'martyr to the drink', as the saying goes. He was also, to some degree, a martyr to the damaged history of Ireland. And I had a part to play in introducing him to that farcical scenario. Who knows to what I subjected him when, in 1982, I took him and the family out of Leeds, where I worked at the university, to live in Ballingeary in the west Cork Gaeltacht? This decision arose out of what was, in me, I now recognise, a state of inanition and despair. I hated living in Leeds, found the university banal and dull and was terrified that our lives were becoming bleak and predictable. I now see that these attitudes were, to a great degree, subjective, reflecting my own unresolved crises at the time, which had to do with unrealised ambitions and thwarted creative impulses. And lack of money. We never seemed to have enough to live on and were always in the red at the bank, in spite of Angela seeking to supplement our income by taking in student lodgers at our end of terrace house in Headingley. It was not possible for her to work; she was trying to bring up four young children, the eldest, Rachel, being at that stage twelve. And, in any case, I used to think, why is it that we do not have enough to live on? Did I not have a good job, a lecturer in a university – the best job anyone had ever had in my family? But every month it was always the same: not enough to live on, even with Angela's lodgers. We lived very frugally, hardly ever went out, drank only on Sunday (a bottle of Moroccan wine with dinner, Sidi Larbi I remember it was called, shared with the lodgers).

One of the reasons we were underpaid, I guess, was that university work at that time was an unbelievably easy ride. I do not think that 'dons' (as we of course liked to think of ourselves), from about 1965 to 1985 or thereabouts, actually did anything remotely resembling work. They enjoyed, rather, a more-or-less continuous leisure, occasionally interrupted by a tutorial or a lecture, and with very little pressure to produce any research. Indeed, if anything, publishing one's work with any degree of avidity at all was regarded as slightly bad form. The odd essay in a journal every five or six years or so was thought of as a fairly hectic pace. Workloads? The term was unheard of, but a 'don' might expect to have perhaps five or six contact hours a week at the most; one of these might be a lecture, the rest would be repeat tutorials, that is, teaching the same stuff to different small groups (no more than four or five in each) of students.

It perhaps sounds idyllic. It was not. University life was, as it perhaps always is, full of rancour and envy. Most of my colleagues longed to get out of Leeds, 'the motorway city of the seventies' as it called itself, and to achieve a fellowship at an Oxford or Cambridge college. Many of them were graduates of those places, and felt they had been passed over in not attaining the laurels of election to the coveted fellowship. In Leeds, and in British universities in general, academics had little to do, but always complained of overwork. They spent huge swathes of time in coffee bars and at lunch. Many drank heavily during the day, taught their few classes (sometimes half-sozzled) and mostly did not bother to write anything at all. Derry (A. N.) Jeffares, the Yeats scholar who appointed me at Leeds, would, when he was in charge there, push them to do research and to introduce new courses. 'You should never teach what you know,' he used to declare confidently; 'much better to learn along with your students.' This declaration used to terrify those 'dons' who only ever wanted to teach their specialism, whereas Derry's view was that you should never teach that, except perhaps at Master's level. Instead, if your subject was English, you should be able to teach anything from Chaucer onwards. However, Derry removed to Stirling in Scotland in 1974, his authoritative and discomfiting urgings were no more, and English at Leeds relaxed.

I was fed up with what I thought was this flatness and complacency, and wanted, desperately, to connect with the life of the Irish language and its culture. I had, you might say, a bad case of cultural nationalism. What is worse: I inflicted this contagion on Angela, then a woman of extraordinary beauty in her early thirties, and on our children. The really clever part of this was that she was to be the one to bear the brunt of my manic plan. I was to commute from Leeds, where I would continue to teach, while she, on her own for most of the time, would bring up the children in a place where they would have contact with their ancestry and their language. Meanwhile I was supposedly devoting myself to scholarship and writing. At the time I could scarcely write prose at all, or only with the most appalling difficulty and effort; and my poetry, if you could call it that, was slack, obscure, and frightened.

Rachel and Killian, our two eldest, even though they had not a word of Irish, went to the Gaelic-speaking primary school in Ballingeary. Full immersion in the language, I thought, would work. Egan went to an Irish-speaking nursery school. Actually all three of them picked up a good deal of Irish, Rachel especially. Egan, named after Aogán Ó Rathaille, one of the last great poets in the integral Gaelic tradition, encountered the Irish form of his name, and one day came home and asked Angela, 'Why is it that I am Aogán Breatnach at school and Egan Welch at home?' An all too Irish question.

What damage was done to him when he was thrust into the culture of Ballingeary, a culture so radically different from that of the suburb of Headingley from which he had been torn? Children are adaptable, we are told, and of course that is true, but they are also susceptible. I have no doubt that Egan experienced, at that very impressionable age, the full impact of the cultural reality that was Ballingeary.

Ballingeary was, and still is, a very beautiful place. It was where the Gaelic League founded, in the early twentieth century, one of its first residential colleges and it became a hallowed place for Cork writers like Frank O'Connor and Sean O'Faolain. It was, O'Connor says, 'the centre' of his Irish world. Teachers of Irish and nationally minded people from all walks of life would come there on holiday in spite of the often terrible weather. It could rain incessantly for weeks, sometimes months, on end, the Cork and Kerry mountains, in the midst of which Ballingeary lay, capturing all the wet winds coming in from the Atlantic. By 1982, when we arrived, it had become what was called a 'breac-Ghaeltacht', a semi-Gaeltacht where Irish and English mixed freely in the daily speech of the local people, with – it should be said – English in preponderance.

It was, to put it bluntly, a culturally mutilated place and community, or rather, a place and people undergoing the ordeal of being transformed from one kind of cultural life into another, while at the same time having profound misgivings about what was happening to them in the process. The silence that would greet you in Shorten's pub when you went in was not just the silence of distrust you can meet in country places anywhere: this silence had an edge of rage in it, a desperation, even a kind of shame. English was almost always spoken in that pub, or, rather, fragments of scornful sentences, comprising mostly mockery and derision, were hurled by one separate drinker to another in thick West Cork accents. Something further removed from the so-called Irish 'craic' would be hard to imagine. These serious imbibers had more in common with the dour drinkers of Glasgow, so brilliantly evoked by the Scottish poet Hugh MacDiarmid, where an urge to conversation or chat is the sign of the flibbertigibbet.

The cultural mutilation, the sense of an ordeal being gone through, was visible in the landscape and environment. There were huge rotting corrugated iron sheds everywhere. The local hotel, Árd na Laoi, where O'Connor and the famous storyteller Timothy Buckley from Gougane Barra used to drink, was closed up, its door-frames falling apart. The little stone-built primary school was replaced by a raw breeze-block affair with an asphalt playground where basketball hoops swung forlornly in the wind and rain. The house we bought, the 'Mill House', had been owned by the Ronans, one of the wealthy families of the area (they were known as the Ballingeary Ewings, after the dynasty in the then popular TV series

Dallas) whose fortunes had declined. The last of the line had been an alcoholic. He had, as my father used to say, pissed a fortune up against the wall. But there was alcoholism everywhere, a dependency facilitated by the poteen made locally in huge quantities in stills fired by gas from the handy, mobile and cheerfully yellow Calor Gas cylinders. Butane was a great boon to the illicit liquor industry.

The Mill House overlooked the mill itself, a great corrugated iron hulk, thrown up on a simple wooden frame in the 1940s, presumably to take advantage of the increased demand for flour during the war years and after. By now it was a rotting dereliction, right in front of us, the view from our front windows. Inside this huge shed was a piece of engineering, very sophisticated in its day, in the form of a great water-powered turbine which drove the millwheels, all stone, in a complicated articulation of cogs, rods, pistons, and flywheels. The turbine was driven by a flow of water from the mountain above and behind the house, which was controlled by a system of connected ponds and small lakes with sluices, so that the water could be held and released as needed. These ponds and little lakes were all on our land.

As well as being a place of dereliction, the house, mill, sheds, and old pig sties were also intriguing and magical. The mill no longer functioned as such (although engineers told me that it could be made to work again and that I could produce my own electricity), but part of the building was used as a retail outlet for a cattle feed business based in Inchigeelagh, six miles up the road. This little shop, open a few days a week, was looked after by a small, neat, excitable man called Johnny Moynihan. Johnny's English was extraordinary, full of elaborate emphasis and declaration, his voice rising often to a near-roar in his anxious need to communicate clearly what was in his mind. His Irish was beautifully lucid and ordered, perfectly judged in its syntax and grammatical precision. A man with two personalities, one hectic and confused, the other poised and relaxed. I have never encountered a more perfect example of the cultural divide in Irish life; he was a walking example of the mutilation of which I speak. He had a slight halt in his leg, there from birth.

Over the mill stream, above one of the moss-lined ponds, stood a statue of St Bernadette. The pond had set into its edge a flat iron plate, from which the water fell in a smooth, translucent curtain of water. Bernadette was kneeling in adoration to another statue, placed slightly higher up, of Our Lady of Lourdes. Over the statue of Our Lady was a curved band of metal with the words 'I am the Immaculate Conception' picked out in blue against white. The statues were also painted blue and white. This arrangement was evidence of the special devotion to Our Lady during the 1930s and 1940s, a devotion still widely in evidence into the 1980s, when it was attested that statues of the Virgin began to move at various shrines in Munster.

Lourdes in the south of France had long been a major site of Catholic pilgrimage, and Bernadette Soubirous was canonised a saint of the church in 1933. The mill would have been built not too long after Bernadette's canonisation. The words above Our Lady's statue are those which Bernadette reported the Virgin to have said to her on 25 March 1858 after she asked the apparition who she was. When the Ronan family built the shrine above the mill, putting it under the protection of Our Lady, they would have been very much aware of the appropriateness of their action: Bernadette's father, François, was a miller.

Across from the little shop and office where Johnny Moynihan conducted his part-time business, there stood a tiny house with two windows and a rickety door. Johnny used it as a store room. Unlike the mill itself, this was a sturdy construction in stone and rendered cement walls with a slated roof. On the right-hand side of the door, set into the rendering, was a small piece of red sandstone cut from the local rock. Inscribed on it, in beautiful and elegant Greek lettering, was the name Seán Mac Cárthaigh. I asked Johnny who this person was, but he did not know. Another neighbour, Seán Lucey, a reserved and silent man given to binges of heavy drinking, told me that the store was a schoolhouse from way back, and that the name beside the door was that of the teacher, a very learned man, who taught Latin, Greek and mathematics, and pre-pared scholars so they could study for the priesthood in Maynooth or on the continent. Seán also told me that Mac Cárthaigh, the hedge-schoolmaster, was a poet, and that he lived at the time of the Famine, or further back.

It was strange to think that here, in the now desolate townland of Kilmore, a quarter of a mile from Ballingeary, Greek was taught in the 1830s or 1840s. Of course at that time, when the sandstone was quarried and inscribed, this townland would have been far from desolate; it would have teemed with people, still part of the old civilisation, relatively undisturbed in this natural fastness created by mountain and the wet boggy land. In a gallery in Edinburgh I once came across an old map of Ireland from the early nineteenth century on which Kilmore was marked, but not Ballingeary.

By the time we came to live there, the area was in decline. The Irish residential summer school, a concrete and tubular steel monstrosity built in the 1960s to replace the one attended by O'Connor, stood empty for most of the year. Already, in the 1980s, it was dilapidated, the perspex awnings on the cycle sheds and walkways loose and cracking in the winter gales. Shorten's pub would have a few desolate drinkers during the day and for the best part of the night until ten o'clock or so, when some of the older folk in the village would drop by. The priest assigned to the church was a straightforward soul whose Irish was atrocious, so that when he said Mass you flinched at his incompetence in the language, a stammering inadequacy the people had to put up with. There were the rotting sheds at Kilmore and all round the village. Money was scarce. Young people were leaving the country in droves, as in the 1950s, going to America, returning to the building sites in England.

The country had had sixty years of (partial) independence at this stage, but there was a strong sense that the experiment had failed. European money had not started to flow in anything like the way it would in the years to come (that would take the brilliance and inventiveness of Charles J. Haughey and other modernisers to achieve); there was a feeling of impoverishment and humiliation. And also, at this time, Northern Ireland was heading into the final bloody convulsions of renewed conflict (explosions, torture, executions, judicial lies) before the peace process began to develop over the next ten years or so. Ballingeary in its desolation, silence and loneliness seemed to embody a dereliction of spirit that came from a history of failure and misdirection, both locally and nationally, as well as from a general incapacity to cope with the pressures of the contemporary world. The Irish language itself, for which Ballingeary had been a centre and a symbol of renewal in the first half of the twentieth century, was now on its last legs. The good cheer and intense courtesy of Johnny Moynihan, with his limping gait, his strange English, his immaculate Irish, his sadness, was a human embodiment of a condition of collective disappointment and inanition.

To all this I exposed Egan. He drank in the sorrow of Ballingeary, its long rainy days, its lonely nights. The Mill House, our family home, was a house of whispers. There was the sound of the stream and waterfall that flowed beneath the image of the Immaculate Conception, but also, in the house itself, a kind of faint susurrus, as of voices on the edge of hearing, a hushed collective chatter. I am not making this up. It was a troubled house. Sometimes I would wake in the morning exhausted, confused as to what I should do that day: write, work in the garden, do some renovation in the house, try to fix up part of the abandoned pig sties up the back which overlooked one of the mill ponds. There was a horrifying amount to do and little sense that there was any point to the daunting effort involved since it all could easily go to waste again in the way that the mill had, and the village itself. This malfunctioning of resolve was not just something in me; I could see it all round me in Ballingeary, in the silences, the inactivity, the cynicism, the mockery of effort, the drinking. Egan was immersed in this cultural and emotional quicksand, and I trace a direct connection between this early experience and his being doomed to becoming a searcher into the root-systems of Celtic tradition, the nature of which remains, to a large extent, inscrutable. And yet at the same time the search compelled him because, if it were possible to discern a connection between your own character and the origins from which it arises, if it were possible to bypass the misdirections and confusion of lived circumstance, then the 'something else' he wrote of in his suicide note might be clarified. The task was hopelessly difficult. It was, to quote (out of context) the seventeenth-century poet Andrew Marvell, 'begotten by /Despair upon Impossibility'.

When Egan died, I received a letter of most tender condolence from an old friend of the Leeds days, the English poet Geoffrey Hill, in which he said that, knowing how much my family meant to me, he could scarcely imagine how terrible this blow was. He went on to say, generously, that he was sure that I had nothing to reproach myself with in respect of how I treated my children, unlike himself, he said. I am certain that in this self-accusation Geoffrey Hill is being unjust to himself, but remorse is not a kind of comforting self-rebuke, it is a flood of shame that overwhelms. And he was wrong about me. I know only too well how my acts and words have, time and again, in sickening repetition, inflicted deep cuts on those I love, and who have had the misfortune to have loved me.

Once, when we were living in Portstewart, I was upstairs writing in a small study that I had when, suddenly, there were ructions below. Egan and Tiernan, 'the boys' as we used to call them (there was only a year between them), were fighting and shouting, and, as their older brother Killian used to say, 'creating haddock'. I lost my temper. I was writing; it probably wasn't going well, and I came down the stairs in a towering rage, loving it, positively cavorting in my anger. Egan would have been about six or seven. I came, roaring with rage, into the dining room where the boys were. There, standing on the red clay-tiled floor, was Egan, frozen in terror. His blond hair was in ringlets around his face, now almost green with fear; his eyes were wide open in panic at the thought of what might lie ahead. The boys knew these rages. I had, of course, studied such things under a master, my own impossibly angry father. Tiernan, strangely, was much less scared of me than was Egan; he was frightened, but not rigid with fear as Egan was.

Egan stood there, hands raised beseechingly as I moved towards him, intending to strike. He asked me not to hit him. 'Please please, Dad, don't. I'm sorry. I'll be quiet.' Something broke inside me. How could I make someone so vulnerable so frightened? I went to him and put my arms around him as he cried against my stomach. Jesus Christ, what beasts we are.

14

The Gunk

I am now writing this on the eve of the first anniversary of Egan's funeral, 11 February 2008. A year has passed. We light candles on his grave overlooking the Bann; we try to keep a light burning there continuously. The headstone will shortly be erected. We go on. People wrote to us, spoke to us, kindly, when he died, to say that time will be a healer. People say those things and do so, rightly, because they need to say something of comfort. But there is no comfort; there can be no release from grief, just that the rawness abates. The sorrow remains, grows steadier if anything. The death of a child changes your life for ever.

I met, in Sainsbury's in Coleraine, our parish priest, Father Charles Keaney, the man who officiated at Egan's funeral. He asked me how we were getting on; I said fine, that the constant pain had gone. 'Yes,' he said, 'but it will come up on you; you'll get the unexpected shock of it, the gunk from nowhere.' Father Keaney knows about such things.

What sometimes comes to me as a gunk is the shock of realisation that Egan is actually dead and gone, that a life has left this world. All that trouble he went to: to gain a mastery of language, enabling him to write wittily and with style; to become a very good guitarist and drummer; to achieve a brilliance and inventiveness in computer technology: all this gathering of knowledge, skill, and experience is now consigned to the grave. Mastery came easily to him. There was no skill or technology that he could not equip himself with if he set his mind to it. Also gone is the love he gave to people, the laughter he brought with him into all kinds of situations when he was not drinking. When he was, grim fixity took over. He had the gift of comedy. I recall him, standing in his blue overalls, ludicrously voluminous on his slender frame, making a comic scene out of painting a bedroom in his new house, the decorator's get-up becoming a farcical costume as he turned the ordinary into helpless hilarity. All this gone. Everyone who loses someone they love thinks the same thing: how can such an excess of life and vitality not be any longer in the world? How is it that the mere drawing of breath can make such a difference? 'But she is in her grave,' writes Wordsworth in one of his 'Lucy' poems, 'and, oh,/ The difference to me'. The depths that these two lines plunge into can scarcely be fathomed. What Wordsworth is registering here, in that 'oh' at the end of the line, is what Father Keaney called the 'gunk'.

The 'gladness' in Egan had its dark side, which showed itself in 'despondency' and what would have been called 'madness'. These words, in quotation marks, come from another poem by Wordsworth, 'Resolution and Independence', which follows a shift of mood from elation to despair. It is as if those who are capable of totally absorbed delight in life have to pay for that gift with an equally strong predilection towards sadness. Egan's life was darkening steadily from around the middle of 2003. His first period of attempted rehabilitation was at Cuan Mhuire outside Newry, an alcohol-treatment clinic run by the Sisters of Mercy, towards the end of the following year. His admittance there was the result of a failed attempt, on my part, to try to change his outlook on life.

In October 2004 an old childhood friend of mine, Lee Nolan, came to visit us in Coleraine with his wife Pauline. As boys in Cork, Lee and I were close friends, where we had a wonderful time devising home-made bombs from gunpowder mixed from ingredients easily bought in chemists' shops. Lee and his grandmother left Cork in the late fifties to settle in London with his mother and her new husband, but he and I never lost touch. While he was staying with us in 2004, he told me he had acquired an interest in a pub in a Norfolk village, which he and a business partner were going to renovate and manage. The village was in the heart of the Broads and the pub had an idyllic situation overlooking one of the fen rivers.

At this time Egan was drinking quite heavily, but I did not think he was in any danger. He was depressed, having been outmanoeuvred by an older, wilier and quite ruthless local businessman in a joint venture that turned out to be very much to his so-called partner's advantage. This disappointment had eaten into Egan's courage, so that when Lee told me of his plans for the pub in Norfolk, I thought this could be a chance for Egan to regain his appetite for work and for business. The place had to be cleaned up and repainted; the kitchen, the cookers, fridges, all needed to be scrubbed and scoured. And then, at the re-launch, Egan could help out in the bar and the kitchen. He loved cooking; this could give him an outlet for his talents.

I asked Lee if he would take Egan on. He agreed. There would be no money involved in the initial stages, but if and when things worked out and the pub was running smoothly, then it might be appropriate to have Egan take a financial interest in the business. Meanwhile I would cover all of Egan's costs for travel and subsistence. Egan was enthused by the idea and travelled back to England with Lee and Pauline, staying with them in their house in Surrey for a few days before going up to Norfolk where Lee's partner, Tom, was already at work on the renovations.

Egan, by all accounts, threw himself into the effort. He painted the bars, re-varnished the floors, scoured out the ovens and fridges, lifted years of impacted grease and dirt, and disinfected and shampooed the carpets. He also, I am afraid, threw himself into drinking in a major way. With hindsight, it was naïve of me to put him into an extremely dangerous environment for someone who was, at the least, very fond of drink. Here he was in a pub, which he had the run of. He discovered hundreds of those small, single-serving bottles of wine in the store, all of them past their sell-by date. Tom told Egan he was free to help himself to them, which he did. As luck would have it, Tom, in his fifties, was a recovering alcoholic who, Egan told us, found this environment too much to handle and had started drinking again. I cannot be sure of what happened exactly, and I am going on Egan's account, but it seems that, after a matter of days, work and drink went in tandem, so that by the evening the renovators were falling around the place, paintbrushes or scrubbing brushes in hand, reeling in a drunken stupor.

About two weeks after he moved to Norfolk, we had a call from Egan telling us that he was afraid to leave his room. He and Tom had fallen out, it appeared, because Tom's girlfriend, herself a drinker, had made a pass at Egan. Tom accused him of making the first move. As he was telling me this, he asked me to listen on the phone. Sure enough, I could hear shouting and threats, a male voice roaring in anger. Egan was terrified that Tom was going to kill him. I told him to get out of the pub, and to stay in a hotel somewhere until he could be rescued. Meanwhile I said I would ring Lee and see if he could help. I was also thinking that Lee might give me a better insight into what was going on.

Lee had an entirely different story. According to him, Egan was out of control. Egan had made a play for the girl, Tom was not drinking, and Egan was doing nothing else. I had no idea what the truth was. I asked Lee if he would go to Norfolk and bring Egan back to Surrey, while Angela made arrangements to go over as soon as she could. I could not travel as I had to chair some panel or other at the university. Lee agreed without hesitation to collect Egan. Angela would bring him home.

As soon as Lee picked Egan up from the hotel, he realised he was in a bad way and took him straight to his doctor in Warlingham when he got back to Surrey. The GP diagnosed Egan as alcoholic, the first time this diagnosis had been made. He said he needed treatment, but also that his intake had been such that he should not think of coming off alcohol straight away. He advised Lee that Egan should be limited to no more than three or four bottles of wine a day. A day! I could hardly believe it when Lee told me this. It seemed that Egan had been, for some considerable time, 'self-medicating' for his depression with alcohol, but the extent of his consumption was horrifying.

While Angela was in Surrey, I went to see our own GP, James Harley, who suggested that I try to get Egan admitted to Cuan Mhuire, that is, James emphasised, if he were willing to go in. When Angela told me on the phone how bad things were, I decided to contact the treatment centre and take the necessary steps towards admission. Egan was utterly in the grip of drink. The experience in Norfolk, which I had hoped would help him re-orient his life, had only sent him deeper into the pit of addiction and mania. All the demons assembled in Norfolk: rage at others and at himself; fear; paranoiac hysteria that Tom and the girlfriend were plotting to have him beaten up; anger at Lee, whom he believed was exploiting him.

What, I often think, were those bleak days in Norfolk like for Egan? I imagine him looking out of the window of his bedroom, a room he is scared to leave because of what he believes is being plotted against him; checking the lock on his door in terror; listening to Tom stomping around the empty pub, roaring in drunken delirium; staring at the brightly coloured flags on the barges and cruisers moored at the canal-bank in the bleak November light. The only relief to be found was in the small, poisonous, screw-topped bottles of out-of-date wine.

There is a photograph of Egan, taken the evening Angela arrived at Lee's. He is playing the guitar to accompany Anna, Lee's daughter, who is singing. His face has the slack and loose grey texture of someone who has been drinking for days. The eyes, as he looks sideways at Anna, have the glazed stare of the addict.

The following night I collected Angela and Egan from the airport. Having made all the preparations, I was taking him straight to Cuan Mhuire. In 2004 Cuan Mhuire was the only place in Northern Ireland where they would admit someone who was drunk; all other places require patients to be sober for at least three or four days. It was just as well that it had such a policy then(they have since had to change it for lack of resources) because when Egan got off the plane he was plastered, staggering all over the place and looking for more drink even before we left the airport. He was insistent that the only way he could face going into this place he knew nothing about was if he were well and truly drunk. I told him we would get him some drink on the way to Newry, but that we really needed to get going: it was now about nine o'clock in the evening, and it would take us at least an hour to get there.

We set off. Egan was rambling and confused, his mind in pieces. All the way down the road he was writhing around in the back seat of the car, pleading for drink. I turned off at Banbridge and went into the little town, now mostly in darkness, looking for an off-licence. I found one and bought what he was looking for, a bottle of Baileys Irish Cream. Maybe, I was hoping, this will be the last thing he will ever drink: the Cuan Mhuire programme is, like most such programmes, based on total abstinence and the twelve steps of Alcoholics Anonymous. But I knew, as I went up to the desk to pay, the heavy brown bottle in my grasp, that this was never going to be. I took it out to the car. Egan unscrewed it and put the neck to his head, gulping back the sweet thick liquor.

It was after eleven when we got to Cuan Mhuire. We drove down to the reception area, parked and went in. The nurse on duty, a good-looking woman aged about forty or so, started the admission process. I had already given some particulars over the phone but there were things she had to check, such as, was Egan coming in of his own free will? She told us she had children of her own, that she worried about them all the time. I was looking around. This was not at all as I had imagined it might be. I thought it would have the air of a hospital, but no, everything was rough-and-ready, as James Harley had said it was. The floors were far from sparkling, the place hadn't been painted in a long while, and there was a lot of beauty board in evidence, that cheap polyurethane false timber that is tacked on battens over surfaces which need to be hidden. There was a chapel into which Angela and I went to pray. Meanwhile, Egan was being personally interviewed by the duty nurse in a separate room. When they came back he was sent off somewhere else for the next stage in the admissions process. And then the kindly nurse said a surprising thing; she said that Egan was a lovely boy but that he was in a bad way. He had, she said, a long road in front of him. We had not realised things were that bad.

Egan was to go into the male detox unit. This was a large room with six or seven beds, all occupied but for the one assigned to

Egan. The person in charge of the unit, a man in his forties, told us that he had been in a bed in the room just a week before, in a terrible state, just like Egan was now. 'You'll be fine in a day or two,' he told Egan; 'you won't know yourself.' 'Really?' said Egan. 'That'll be something to look forward to.' He laughed, eager to please, as ever, wanting not to be any trouble. Even in these circumstances, he was laughing and smiling, full of courtesy. I thought my heart would break as I looked at him. What terrible things the world does to those who are gentle.

I looked around at the dismal room: the cheap metal-frame beds, hospital rejects by the look of them, covered with old eiderdowns and duvets; the naked bulbs in the sockets overhead; the scraps of furniture by the bedsides; the plastic ashtrays; the shapes in the beds, some sleeping, some looking on in pity at this young man and his distraught parents, knowing the nature of suffering to the bone. I looked at the man who was taking care of Egan and felt a huge wave of love and gratitude for the people in this place, the patients and those who ran it. This is a place of hope, I thought. Cuan Mhuire means the Harbour of Mary. This was a harbour, truly, a place of refuge, the harbour of the Mother of God.

When Sister Consilio Fitzgerald, a Kerrywoman, founded the first Cuan Mhuire in Athy, Co. Kildare in 1965, she had no money. A farm came up for auction which she thought would suit her purposes. She went along to her bank manager to ask for an overdraft, so she could make the bid. He asked her what collateral she could offer and how she would find the cash to meet the cost of repayments on what she wanted to borrow. She answered that Our Lady would be the collateral, and that She would also provide the means whereby the loan (because that was what they were talking about) would be repaid. He sanctioned the overdraft, and Sister Consilio met the stipulated repayment schedule. The nun had spoken the truth: Our Lady did provide. Can you imagine having Our Lady accepted as security for a loan these days? There are now five such treatment centres, harbours for the afflicted, across the island of Ireland.

The duty nurse came in and gave Egan his medication, drugs to ease the body's withdrawal from alcohol. He went to sleep. Gratefully we watched him at rest. The nurse said we could go and we set off for Coleraine, hoping for the best. Over the next four weeks we visited Egan every weekend and there were visits too from Rachel and her husband, Richard. Angela and I would take him out to lunch in Newry, during which he would drink coffee. He was generally in good spirits, but there was always a sadness behind his cheerfulness. I had the sense all the time that he was going through a series of motions, doing what was expected of him. I knew his heart was not in this. We would go back to Cuan Mhuire in the late afternoon on these visiting days and would have tea in the day room, which was served in thick white mugs by a big middle-aged man, built like a boxer. He was an alcoholic and had been in Cuan Mhuire for years having discovered that he was unable to cope in the world outside, where he could not do without drink. This hulking gentle creature who, as he handed you your twenty pence cup of tea, would make of it a gesture of love, was allowed to stay inside and work at odd jobs like this for his keep. He would wipe down the formica tables, mop the scuffed wooden floor, top up the coal-burning stove from a scuttle, keep control of the remote for the TV.

Everyone smoked, practically all the time. Off the day room was a smoking room, always packed with smokers, sitting crammed on low long stools, of the kind you used to see in school assembly halls. As well as the weekend visits, there were also family days, when the patients and their relatives would be addressed together, and the nature of the treatment programme outlined. At the heart of that programme were the twelve steps of Alcoholics Anonymous. It was also made clear that alcoholism was an illness, not a weakness, and that those who loved alcoholics should not 'facilitate' their drinking. Nor should we try to persuade them to stop. That must come from their own desire to change, which would be prompted by the grace of God, if it was his divine will. On one occasion we were addressed by Sister Kathleen, who ran the Newry unit. She said, of drinkers, that they were usually very gifted and sensitive people. In fact, she said, they are the nicest and most generous people you could ever meet, but they do not believe that they have any value, they do not see that they are loved by Christ, that they are unique.

'And that,' she said, 'is what we do here. We try to show them that they are loved by Our Lord Jesus Christ and that he will never fail them.'

Egan came out of Cuan Mhuire in early December 2004, slightly early; not a good sign. Within days he was drinking again. On Christmas Eve he was beaten up by Lundy once more, this time without his sidekick Myler, in the toilets of a bar in Coleraine, ending up in A & E until the small hours of the morning. At Christmas dinner the following day (dry for all of us, including his maternal grandfather, his sister and brothers, and their partners, all back for the 'festive' season) he was covered in bruises, had a black eye and a number of stitches to his head. It was a miserable affair. In the New Year he was back in Cuan Mhuire, and in that year, 2005, his long decline began to accelerate.

15

The Axe Falls

The Otherworld, to which drink promises access, has, as has been said, many names in Irish. One of them, Tír fó Thoinn, means the Land Under the Wave. Egan finally went there, a place for which in some sense he had longed, in the small hours of 28 January 2007, a Sunday morning.

On the day before, Angela and I called, as had been arranged, at his house on Brook Street to take him to the Lidl supermarket on the outskirts of Coleraine. It was mid-afternoon. He was freshly shaved and showered, and smelled strongly of aftershave, which rang alarm bells. When he lived with us, Egan would often heavily douse himself in cologne to disguise the reek of drink. In particularly bad times he would drink the stuff as well. His face was slightly flushed too, another bad sign. He was on Antabuse, the prescription drug that produces a very severe reaction to alcohol if it is drunk while taking this medication. I had seen the reactions to drinking on Antabuse before and Egan looked as if he was suffering a mild version of these now. He was flustered and agitated as he gathered up his things. We said hallo to the cat he adored, called by him Parsnipia, to suggest the homely vegetable as well as some Roman Empress. We still have her. After he died she was confused and seemed to mourn him for months.

I was watching him nervously all the time. There were no definite signs of drink and yet when we went out and he pulled the

PVC door behind him and checked if it was locked, he staggered slightly. But there was not about him that air of elaborate carefulness the drunk has as he or she is trying to negotiate simple manoeuvres without giving themselves away. We got into the car, Egan sitting in the back seat, holding a clutch of plastic bags for the shopping. We drove down his street, turned left onto the Millburn Road and past the house where I am now writing this, the last time he would go past the house alive. The next time he would go past he would be in his coffin.

Egan was in good form as we drove to the supermarket. My anxiety about his condition calmed a bit as it became clear that whatever the cause for the agitation was, it was not drink-induced. He was chatty, easy in himself, telling us that Charlotte, his fiancée, was going out that night with her mother, that she would stay over in Portstewart, that he would watch a couple of DVDs. I thought how hard this was for him. He could not go out with the girl he loved and with her mother, because there would be drink, and that was out of the question.

Looking back now, it is clear that the confusion and upset I saw in him was caused by the Diazepam he would have taken to calm himself before our visit and the trip to the supermarket. Ordinary day-to-day meetings and engagements often threw him into a panic, and when he could not have recourse to drink, he took this hellish stuff, which he was getting from Karachi via the internet. Some months later, cleaning out his house after he died, I found hundreds of these pills under the cushions of his sofa in the living room, still in their bubblewrap, inside envelopes posted from Pakistan. I did not fully realise it until he died, but Egan was afraid of everything. He needed Diazepam to take the brute edge off things as they are.

And yet, in spite of this continuous fear, he loved life, and he loved shopping. When we got to the supermarket Egan headed quickly for the fruit and vegetable section, loading up with onions, garlic, cucumber, carrots, cauliflower, tomatoes; then apples, lots of them, and other fruit. When not drinking Egan would eat as many as ten or twelve apples a day, and he loved the big red American ones they had at Lidl. He chose, making a comic routine out of the business, a huge pack of shredded wheat, and a twelve-pack of long-life milk. We then ambled, Egan pushing the laden trolley, over to the hardware and clothing section, with its cheap rubber boots, packs of underwear, pillows, extension ladders, telescopes, garden seats, fishing rods. The previous July I'd bought him, at this very store, a German fly-fishing kit, with fly reel, floating line, traces, flies, the works, all in a neat plastic carrier with a handle attached. He and I had fished together one sultry late afternoon at a pond stocked with rainbow trout near Ballyrashane Presbyterian Church outside Portrush, and as we fished we could hear a local marching band playing as it wended its way through the country lanes, the sounds fading and increasing as the direction of the warm breezes changed. I recall Egan casting the fly-line uncertainly, and thinking how great was his longing to belong to a world in which he was destined to be a stranger. The drums and the music were, somehow, beautiful and remote, messages from that world he longed to belong to.

At the supermarket checkout, Egan separated his purchases from ours while engaging in friendly chat with the girl behind the till, a tall, dark-haired girl with a pale, exhausted face, who knew him. So many people knew him. I wanted to buy an axe to chop some wood, and there was a B&Q outlet in the retail park, but Egan asked me to take him back home. Charlotte was coming round before going out that night, and he wanted to be there when she came. We drove to Egan's house, past the Catholic church on Laurel Hill, down Somerset Drive, Coleraine's own drug-pushing area where he'd been beaten up by Myler and Lundy, past the Taj Palace takeaway from where he would order his scorching vindaloos and phals two or three nights a week, across the Old Bridge over the Bann, past Dunnes, then up Union Street where he been set upon by the same two thugs, then left down Brook Street. His last arrival at his house, his last drive around the town.

Always the host, he asked us in for tea. Charlotte arrived shortly after us and she had brought a cheesecake, his favourite. Tea was made. Meanwhile, I browsed through some CDs of films he had burned for me, among them copies of *The Black Dahlia* and *Talladega Nights*. He was always doing things like this to please us. One time I told him how much I liked the music of Jimmy Smith, the great exponent of the jazz Hammond organ, whose visceral sound he seemed to haul from the entrails of the instrument. Two days later Egan arrives with half a dozen albums of Jimmy Smith's, which he has downloaded, presenting them to me in a CD folder with separate pockets for each disc, the title of each one written on it in his own hand. I have them still, still play them, and will keep them as long as I live.

He cut slices of the cheesecake to go with the tea. The day was dark, overcast, a typical late January day. Charlotte was going out, as were Angela and I. Egan knew he was on his own that night, condemned to solitude by his addiction. We left, Charlotte staying behind. He saw us to the door, stood there as we drove off, smiling and waving at us for the last time.

I still wanted to get the axe. We drove back out to B&Q, with its garish orange décor and lofty aisles, the huge bays stacked with timber, garden machinery, lighting, paint, tiles, bathrooms. I found a good heavy axe, the head enclosed in a button-down plastic pocket, and carried it out to the till. On the way there we met friends of ours, Tom and Sylvia Clarke. I made a silly, mock-threatening gesture with the axe, holding it up as if for combat. Tom, responding to this pantomimic carry-on, cowered in mock fear. We exchanged pleasantries. Tom and Sylvia were also going out that night, as they always did on a Saturday. There was a lightsome, weekend feeling. We went home and got ready. I had a couple of drinks to set me up and was glad to be able to do so, seeing as Egan was in his own house. Or so I thought. As I would have been having these pre-dinner drinks, he was drinking his way to his death.

16

Brigid of Kildare

The next day, Sunday, Angela and I went to Mass at St John's Church across the river. Afterwards I cooked breakfast. Around noon there was a call from Charlotte. Was Egan with us? Had we seen him? She had been trying to call him all morning, but his mobile kept switching to answerphone. Angela decided she would go around to his house. When I offered to go along with her, she said she wanted to go on her own. I agreed to this, being in a state of locked fear as to what was waiting for us in the hours to come. In the grim light I went out to the garden to chop wood with the new axe. I knew, as I lifted the axe to split the first of the logs, that he was gone.

Angela spent hours in the house on Brook Street. She made tea, tidied up a bit, put away the day before's shopping that was still sitting on the kitchen table, talked to the cat, and prayed. It is her way to pray against what may be coming. I prayed too. I was chopping up large segments of a cherry tree left over after it had been cut down a month or two before. Egan had arranged for the tree surgeon – someone he knew – to come. There was a large cylinder of trunk that I stood upright and on this I placed the smaller sawn pieces to be riven. I would up-end them and bring down into the grain the heavy head of the orange-handled axe. More often than not, with each downward drive, the two split segments would fly apart, separating cleanly. The light was dark and grey, full of moisture, but there was no rain. I worked with every effort I could muster. Sometimes, on the stroke, the axe would bite into a knot in the chunk of wood, and stick there, lodged, and then I would have to lift the whole piece, with the axe embedded, into the air and bring it all back down on to the chopping block, driving the iron deeper into the thickened wood on the knot. Eventually the impacted growth would give and the wood would split open, releasing the smell of old sap, the perfume of the years, strong and sweet in the heavy air.

At each stroke I prayed to Christ, to the Virgin, to St Joseph, Jesus's long-suffering and patient father, that Egan would come back to us. But all the time I knew he was gone. I do not know what I felt that afternoon: I was just going through whatever it was I was going through as I gathered the split logs and stacked them in the garage and the summerhouse.

It was 28 January 2007. Egan had been due to be born in February 1980. Angela had had, since childhood, a dread of the month of February, a month during which she felt bad things happened, and she was relieved when Egan was born so effortlessly on 31 January, missing February by a hair's breadth. And the following year, after she had become pregnant again with our youngest, Tiernan, she was delighted when he too bypassed the February date he was due on, hanging on until 1 March 1981.

The first day of February is, in Ireland, the feast day of St Brigid, a Christianised pagan deity, closely associated with Kildare town, where her cult appears to have had one of its centres. Kildare means oak wood (dair is Irish for oak; doire, as we saw with Derry, is an oak-grove), and the name preserves in the 'dr' sound a link with 'druid', the same link that Derry has. This place name, Kildare, reminds us once again, as with Egan's tree from the Diamond in Coleraine, of the association of oaks with druidism and nature worship. The pagan deity Brigantia was the tutelary goddess of a tribe known as the Brigantiae who occupied parts of northern Britain as well as Leinster. When Christianity was established at Kildare, it absorbed her cult and made her into a saint known in Irish folklore as Bridget, 'the Mary of the Gael'.

Angela's mother, Bridget Malone, was called after the saint. She believed, as did a great many people(my mother among them) that on St Brigid's Eve, the last night of January, the saint roved abroad to herald the beginning of spring. Women left out a piece of cloth on a thorn bush, a tree or on a nail, for the saint to touch. This rag would then be used as protection against illness or the evil eye; sometimes pieces of it would be sewn into a girl's clothing to protect her virginity; or it would be waved over a cow if it was having trouble calving. The first of February, the beginning of Brigid's month, was, in pagan times, one of the main feast days of the Celtic calendar, and was called Imbolc, a term connected with lactation, the arrival of milk in the udders of ewes for the lambing season.

February was regarded as a month of transition, from winter into spring, death into life, which explains the special place accorded it in Celtic belief and the fear and awe it evoked in Irish country people, an attitude of mind still very much in evidence in the way Angela regarded it. Certainly for her, and for our family, the month of February 2007 was to be a dreadful time.

As I was chopping logs on the last Sunday of January, Angela sat in the living room of Egan's house dying, as they say, many deaths. It is often the fate of women to have to wait. Now her deeply wounded and troubled boy had been missing for nearly twenty-four hours, and it wasn't like him not to make contact. He knew how much she worried about him and he would always get in touch to let her know where he was, even in his most drunken state. I kept on ringing her until she asked me to stop. 'What is the point?' she said. She would let me know if there were any news and in any case, each time the phone rang it raised her hopes it might be him. She was, she said, praying that he was in someone's house, somewhere like Janet's perhaps, a drinking den, holed up in the company of the 'bottom feeders' (as his sister called them) whom he sometimes mixed with.

A mother's love is compounded with fear. Unconditional love, such as a mother has for her child (there are exceptions, we know), involves fear, because there is no escape from whatever brutalities fate chooses to inflict. The world is full of possible mischance: a child may fall off a cliff, may get mangled in a car accident as he cycles home from school for his lunch on a sunny day (as happened to a cousin of mine), may be taken advantage of, be bullied or experience harassment at work. Angela waits in fear in the living room of the house we have helped Egan to buy, sitting on the black imitation-leather sofa he picked up in a second-hand furniture store in Ballymoney for a few pounds. She waits.

Later in the afternoon Angela made her way back from Brook Street through the darkening air. I was still chopping the cherry wood, gathering up the blocks, stacking them in aromatic piles. I recall seeing her walk up the side of the house, then along the narrow path by the summerhouse, which Egan had rebuilt with someone called Steve Kirk in another of his failed ventures, Welch and Kirk Developments. This was the starting project and they made a brilliant job of it. But it was not to be. Egan, I later found out, would start drinking in the morning while they were on a job, and he was leading Steve down the same road. Steve, of about Egan's age, had sense and bailed out.

Angela is coming up past the summerhouse on a pathway made of engineering brick some time in the 1920s or 1930s, a pathway Egan cleared for me in May 1998 when he left school, with my consent, not having taken his A levels. I can see by Angela's tired walk, her pale face, that she too knows he is gone. She is walking with the ancient shuffle all women have who are afflicted by grief, the walk that would have been seen in the streets of Troy after it was burned; on the Blasket Islands as the women came back from the harbour in storm, their menfolk missing; at Srebrenica in Bosnia.

We go inside, we have tea. It is too early to call the police; Egan has been missing for not quite twenty-four hours, and they are reluctant to become involved in a missing person investigation before then, on the reasonable grounds that most people who disappear without explanation turn up within that time frame. We say to ourselves that there is a chance that he is alright, that he will phone and say he is sorry; can we come and get him from some drinking hole? But the computer in his house was left turned on; the electric fire was burning and, because he paid for his electricity by top-up card which has to be bought, it is unlikely he would leave the power on if he were intending to be out for any length of time. He had said he was planning to watch a couple of films, and Charlotte told us when she rang after she'd left him that he was on the point of going to the rental store.

I cannot write about what dark agony Angela went through. For myself, I was just concentrating on practicalities: when should we call the police? Who could we ring that might know where he had been? I drove around the town a few times, looking for Egan. I called a taxi driver called Billy Clugston with whom he had become friends. Billy used to taxi him in his glory days, when he was rolling in cash; the last time he was admitted to Cuan Mhuire, I could not drive him down and we got Billy to do it, Angela going along as well. Billy is a powerhouse of intelligent and forceful energy. He is covered in tattoos and is a chain smoker. With the build of an all-in wrestler, and even though he is in his fifties now, he is still a creature to be reckoned with. When I ring Billy, I ask him to look out for Egan as he drives round, and also to make a few discreet enquiries. Billy has an extensive and complicated network of connections which extends through all strata of Coleraine life. People know and fear him. He is someone very useful to have on your side, and he liked Egan. 'He's a good lad,' Billy said many times, 'too good for the scum he hangs around with.'

Not that Egan had much to do with the drug scene, the pushers, the mules who carry the stuff, for some time now, that we knew of. Those connections had ceased, we believed, as did Charlotte (who would know) from around the time he had gone into St John of God's in Dublin in March the previous year. This meant that there was no point in me contacting any of those he would have fraternised with at one time to see if they knew where he was or might be. The fact was that, apart from Charlotte, his mother and me, there were not many people with whom Egan had contact. And this was why, every day, when he would not be drinking, he would meet Angela after she finished work. They would go for coffee and tea, he asking for four shots of espresso so he would get the coffee hit. After he died, people would remark to Angela how often they would see them around the town together, an odd couple, she a middle-aged woman with bright red hair, he a young man with a shaved head, always deep in conversation, he invariably animated, she laughing, delighting in the wonderful creature her son was when he was sober.

That evening Charlotte came round. I cooked dinner; we drank a lot of wine. I produced a bottle of Talisker malt from the Isle of Skye, and Angela and Charlotte finished it between them.

The following morning, there was still no news. Angela and I went to Coleraine police station to report him missing, supplying the necessary details to the interviewing officer: time last seen, last contact, a photograph. The search began at his house, then ours. This was routine, we were told: missing persons often hide out on their own premises or at the houses of relatives. There were announcements on the local radio and it got into the *Belfast Telegraph* that a 'vulnerable person' (the police phrase, code for alcoholic or addict) was missing, last seen at around six o'clock on Saturday evening.

Straight away the media hyenas moved in. A couple of newspapers got in touch to see if we wanted to tell 'our story'. It would be, we were told, therapeutic. Would we do an interview and be photographed? Did we wish to make a statement? These journalists were just trying to do their job and this was the kind of story that would appeal to readers. The elements were attractive: a good-looking young man is missing; there is a beautiful fiancée; tragedy (drink, which they would have known about by now) lurks in the background; a middle-class family (father a university dean, mother a Citizens Advice Bureau manager, well-known in the town) is touched by the dark wing of fate. This would make a decent story. It might run for a bit.

We refused the offers. Had we accepted them there would have been, given our confused and distracted state, the temptation to speak beyond what would be appropriate; to tell perhaps of the different stays at Cuan Mhuire; the hospitalisations and treatments in County Mayo; the time at St John of God's outside Dublin.

17

The Duke of Ferrara

St John of God's is a mental health hospital outside Dublin, specialising in the treatment of alcohol, drug dependency, eating disorders, and depression. It was founded in 1882 and is run by the
Brothers Hospitallers of St John of God. John of God was a Portu-
guese saint, born in 1495, who, after a period as a fighting soldier,
went insane and ended up in an asylum. Through the prayers and
practical interventions of a spiritual mentor he recovered and
decided to devote his life to caring for the sick poor. Alongside its
charitable function, the Order he founded is also entrusted with
looking after the health of the Pope.

The Order's hospital at Stillorgan is, in Ireland, the equivalent of
The Priory in England, with the difference that many of the
patients at St John of God's are people of modest means. This
cannot be said of The Priory, or the world-famous Desert Canyon
Treatment Centre in Arizona where the clients, many of them
celebrities, tend to be rich. The health service in the Republic of
Ireland leaves a great deal to be desired, but in some respects it
functions effectively. In Ireland you have to pay about sixty euro
when you see your GP, unless you hold a medical card issued to
those in receipt of state benefit or welfare. Hospitalisation can be
free, but there are admission charges, which again are lifted if the
patient is on benefit. However, because the idea of paying for

medical care is accepted, a great number of not especially well-off people pay medical insurance, giving them access to private health-care when they need it. This works in the Republic of Ireland because enough people subscribe to private health schemes to keep the premiums affordable even for those on average incomes. Fur-thermore, many employers assist with employee medical insur-ance. Such a system is quite unlike that which obtains in the United Kingdom, where the prevailing view is that health care is something that should be provided by the state for all, irrespective of their financial position. This means that the National Health Service is charged with taking care of the medical and health-support needs of the great majority of the population, most of whom hold it as a self-evident truth that a citizen should not have to pay for medical treatment. The NHS is greatly loved by the British and it is admired throughout the world. Brought into being by Aneurin Bevan, the Welsh Labour politician, in July 1948, in the teeth of fierce opposi-tion, it is a magnificent institution and still survives in spite of steadily increasing costs as the population of the United Kingdom lives longer, and as ever more sophisticated drugs combat one-time killer diseases.

In Ireland the situation is quite different, where there is a wide-spread culture of medical insurance, and private and publicly funded health care systems interact, not always easily. However, a relatively inexpensive insurance premium will ensure availability of treatment at St John of God's for people with modest incomes. There is nothing like it in the United Kingdom. There are places like The Priory on the one hand, reserved for those with money and, on the other, there are establishments like Cuan Mhuire, rough and ready places, surviving as best they can as charities and on what may be squeezed out of (not always sympathetic) local authorities. Why should such places be funded separately when there is the NHS? This frequently is the response to special provision for alco-hol and drug addiction. And yet when you raise the issue of such dependency in mental health centres, they will quickly tell you that they are not there to deal with addiction and refer you to counsel-lors specialising in this branch of treatment. You then wait for two or three months before you see one of these counsellors, who, more often than not, turns out to be someone with a degree or post-graduate diploma in advice or counselling, not a qualified doctor or psychotherapist. The next appointment will be in another month, by which time the addict is almost certainly back on what he or she craves, driven to it, in part, by the indifference of a futile and overloaded system. Essentially the message is: addict, heal thyself, or die.

There was one terrible afternoon in the summer of 2005. Egan had had his awful Mayo sojourns. He was drinking all the time. He would stay in bed a good part of the day, waiting for us to come home so we could bring him drink; but of course he was drinking all the time from hidden caches about the place, in the attic, or in the loft above the garage. This particular afternoon he was in bed, racked with sorrow and remorse, hating what he was doing to us, yet unable to stop. His mother was with him, trying to comfort him in his misery. I joined them. I had tried to write something for him, a kind of prayer, a statement of fellow feeling, and I brought it in and showed it to him. Muddled by drink, he could not read it. Normally he had an intellect of razor sharpness. I read the piece, a poem in which I join his suffering to that of the great Italian Renaissance poet Torquato Tasso who went insane, who endured the cruel racking of remorse. I explained to him what was intended, and about Tasso, that he came from Sorrento, that in Ferrara he was looked after by the Duke Alfonso d'Este. During this he was sitting up in the bed, pillows behind him. The afternoon sun was shining through the window, emphasising his pale face, the white flakes of eczema on his shaven scalp. His eyes were unfocused and he kept on shifting about in the bed. And then, having listened to the tale of Tasso's sorrow, and of the kindness of Duke Alfonso, he broke down and said, 'Why is it that there is no support? I need help, and there is none.' This, I am sorry to say, is so often the reality of the National Health Service when it comes to the treatment of addiction. You had best look to yourself and your own resources. Which is why, eventually, we sought out particulars of admission to St John of God's.

Egan did not have health insurance, and in any case insurance in Northern Ireland would not cover treatment in the Republic. I had enquired about the cost of a course of treatment at St John of God's around Christmas 2005, from which time we had been discussing with Egan the possibility of his going there. It worked out at about £9,000. We put it to Egan that this sum, or thereabouts, was the money we had found for Rachel to help her buy her first house in Belfast; it was also, roughly, what we gave Tiernan when he set himself up in a house in Leicester; and it was what I had intended doing for Egan as well, and for Killian too. So that, if he wished, he could, as it were, call this sum down now and use it to help get himself well in Dublin. He had found out that Shane McGowan of The Pogues had been a patient at St John of God's and this appealed to Egan. It sounded like a cool place. McGowan is a famous and famously alcoholic singer who seems, amazingly, to be able to perform live on stage while drunk, who has endured various collapses of the liver and other functions, and who yet seems to be able to recover and get on with the chaos of his life and art.

Egan considered this option for a number of months. I now think that he feared he was not ever going to recover, so that such an expense could well be a waste of money. However, in March 2006, while he was living in his flat in Ballymoney, he decided to go.

For five or six months before this, Egan had been through hell. This was perhaps his worst period, from the time in Mayo to his admission to St John of God's. During these months he had taken up with Julie, the girl he had met in the Ross Thomson Unit in Coleraine. Although very ill herself, she was also someone of impressive determination, courage and clarity of mind. When they were discharged from the Ross Thomson, at around the same time, she organised not one, but two flats in Ballymoney, about six miles south of Coleraine, for herself and for Egan, next door to each other. She had decided it would be best if they had separate places, and that it would also be a good thing if they were some distance from their parents. Hers were in a village outside Ballymoney. Egan's flat was a small, dark, pokey cave of a place, with two rooms and a bathroom, but it was clean and recently renovated. There was a great surge of excitement and hope on everyone's part in getting all this arranged, and he and Julie rejoiced in buying their scraps of furniture from a second-hand store round the corner from where they were to live.

Egan's flat became, however, a place of utter dereliction of soul, of unspeakable shame and torture. He was to endure the most abysmal darkness of spirit in these three rooms. The narrow horizontal rectangle of his bedroom window faced a dark concreted entryway into an enclosed yard at the back of the flats, where the bins were kept and clothes lines stretched between galvanised steel poles. One time, when we called round to see him, we looked through this narrow slit of a window to see him spread out on the bed, asleep, we hoped, but we were not sure. We knocked at the door to try to rouse him, and rattled and shouted at the window, but he did not stir. Eventually, not knowing what else to do, I smashed through the front door, and saw food strewn everywhere, cat shit trodden into the laminated floor, cigarettes piled high in the ashtrays, vomit in the bathroom, blood on the walls. We got him up and gave him tea. Wrapped in his filthy dressing gown, he sat in the cheap mock-leather sofa he had bought, watching me as I swept up the detritus of several days drinking and swabbed the floor as best I could. When he was younger, my use (overuse probably) of the word 'detritus' amused Egan greatly and he would delight in deploying it himself in a half-mocking way. It was a word he loved. Now the actuality of it was evidence of a life gone out of control.

One night in Ballymoney, drunk out of his mind (Julie was away, either in hospital or at her parents), he staggered next door to where a girl, someone he would greet when he passed her in the street, lived. He told her he needed help. Why he did not call us I do not know. We may have been away; he often took to the bottle if we were travelling. In any case, this girl, Sandra, decided she would call the minister of her church, Trinity Presbyterian in Ballymoney. The Reverend Ian McNie turned out to be a man of astounding goodness.

Ian McNie came round immediately, even though this would have been about eleven or twelve o'clock at night. Sandra introduced him to Egan and Ian and he talked for an hour or more, the older man listening to the drunken complaints, Egan grateful for someone to talk to, as he always was when in the grip of drink. I learned later that he told Ian of his failures in business, how he had been tricked, how he had made a lot of money and how he had lost it. From that night on, Ian and Egan were very close. The Reverend McNie, a true and faithful Christian, never once judged Egan and treated him, always, with dignity and compassion.

One small incident illustrates this. Ian got a call from a drunken Egan one afternoon. Ian went round, tidied up a bit as Egan lay on the sofa, smoking, and drinking whatever little was left. He was in no condition to venture out, and Ian offered to walk up to the small supermarket nearby and get some of the Cornish pasties or mincemeat pies Egan liked when he had his drink-hunger on him. No, Egan said, it was drink he needed, not food. Now here was a dilemma: the Reverend McNie, minister of Trinity Presbyterian, the church where the great James Armour (famous for his liberal attitudes and saintly life in the early 1900s) had been minister before him, who had never allowed an alcoholic drink to pass his lips in his life, was being asked to go to the off-licence to fetch drink for a bed-ridden alcoholic. Everyone knew Reverend McNie. If he did what Egan asked, he would be seen carrying the telltale blue plastic bags along the street. He would give scandal: before you would know it, the gossip on the street would be that he had been seen carrying drink. No, he could not do that, as much as he wanted to oblige Egan. I should say, by the way, that Egan, like many drinkers, had the ability to persuade you to his point of view, to make you feel that refusal to do as he asked was not an option.

For a while, Ian told me, he thought he should go up the street. Would not that be what Christ would have done? In confusion, he rang Angela, going outside to make the call: by now our families had become friends. He told her he did not think he could go and get the drink himself, but what did Angela think of this as a possible solution? There was a member of his congregation who was a known drinker, a good man but very fond of the booze. Perhaps he could ask this person to carry out Egan's request as an act of charity, a gesture of service to the Lord? Angela pointed out to Ian that supplying drink to an alcoholic is like handing a gun to a man in the last days of cancer. We had learned by now that those who love alcoholics should not supply them with drink. This was something we had done many times, but at this stage we had resolved not to do so again, even though it was difficult to resist his pleadings. In any case, no matter what the difficulty, alcoholics will always find a way of getting their hands on what they crave. Angela told Ian that he should not give in to Egan. She also reminded him that there was, in spite of the sad mania of Egan's need, a funny side to the situation. 'Think,' she said, 'of the excitement you'd cause amongst the most devout members of your congregation if they thought you had this secret vice, now at last breaking cover. You'd become very interesting to them.' Ian laughed the laughter of the saint. He did not provide the drink and Egan, somehow managing to get his hands on what he wanted, continued in his drunken state for another few days.

Ian worked (that *is* the word) very hard with Egan. When he was sober again, Ian had him design the church's website, oversee the installation of a new amplification system and assist at a barbecue for the young members of the congregation. For Egan's birthday that year, Ian took him, along with other young people from the church, to a go-kart race track, an experience he loved. Ian was, I know, trying to win him back for Christ. I prayed he would succeed. Was there a chance Egan would join Ian's congregation? Was there even a wild and remote chance that he would receive a calling from God and become a minister? Should this miracle occur, I knew Egan would be a true follower of Christ. He loved the weak, the poor and the helpless. His own affliction had ensured that he did not have a hard heart. I know Ian and Egan discussed the Bible a great deal, Egan buying his own copy in an expensive edition with detailed commentaries that Ian had recommended. They also considered the option I had raised with Egan, of going into St John of God's. I had explained to Ian how I had put the matter, that the money was available, as a kind of inheritance, if Egan wished to use it in that way. It had to be a free choice. While I am sure Ian never tried to influence the decision, I have no doubt that their discussions were part of the process that finally led to the moment of choice.

18

One in Sixteen

We arrived at St John of God's late in the evening on 7 March 2006 after a long drive from Ballymoney. We had discussed the admission and our approximate time of arrival with the hospital the day before. Egan, in preparation for admission, had not taken a drink for a few days, but was sedated with Librium on his doctor's prescription, to allay the symptoms of withdrawal. As soon as we came through the stained-glass doors into the lobby, with its oak panels and polished flooring, I realised we were in a different environment from any place of treatment he had been in before. The person behind the reception desk was on the phone. Standing in front of it was a tall, good-looking priest who turned and smiled at us and asked us how we were doing. We told him we had come to have our son admitted. The priest immediately shook Egan's hand and wished him well, saying he had come to the right place. Relief flooded through me. There was here again, as in the Noone's house in County Mayo, a renewal of hope.

We were taken to an admissions room where a matron went through the procedures. All the necessary papers were examined: GP reports, medical files, prescriptions; and the cheque for the full cost of the treatment and accommodation was handed over. There were, we were told, no refunds if a patient decided to leave before the completion of the programme in thirty days. There was a long waiting list for each bed in the hospital and this opportunity, the matron told Egan, was not to be wasted. Was he certain, she asked, that this was something he wanted to embark upon. It was, he said.

We were then shown to his bedroom along carefully waxed and polished parquet floors: you could smell the lavender. His room was carpeted and the bed was freshly made with the crisp linen sheets turned down. The light was soft and muted. There was a TV. When we came out, we saw a little knot of patients sitting around a table, drinking tea and eating lemon cake. Half the round of the cake remained on the table. The nurse told us it was somebody's birthday. Soon Egan would be seen by a doctor, she said, who would give him something to help him sleep through the night. Then he could get something to eat in the dining room, which was still open. It stayed open, we were told, until well after midnight; people were being admitted all the time and they often had to come a long way, as we had. We stayed with Egan until he was shown in to the doctor; then we left for our overnight hotel.

Egan stayed at St John of God's for the full term. Each week there was a family day when relatives or loved ones visited patients. These days were, we had been told, an important part of the treatment, because they were meant to involve those closest to the addict in the process of self-examination and renewal that would, we all hoped, lead to healing and to a changed life. The family involvement was also a means whereby the alcoholic was confronted with the consequences of his or her drinking in the lives of others. The programme had iron in it. Its approach involved confronting the alcoholic, steadily and throughout the duration of the programme, with the damage addiction does to the addict and to those who happen to love him or her.

By Egan's account, patients were confronted with other realities also. He told us they were given a terrifying statistic: that only one in sixteen alcoholics remained sober for any significant length of time; that even fewer stayed off it for good. The odds, he was told, were stacked against anyone with this illness. I actually find it hard to believe that this was said. It is at least doubtful, to my mind, that patients on a programme in which they all had invested hope as well as money, were told that it was not, almost certainly, going to work, that they were, most of them, under a sentence of death. No, what I now think happened is that Egan, who had a rigorously analytical brain, had worked out what the survival statistics were for him. He would, I believe, have assessed the nature of his own dependency against the accounts he would have had, directly from those he shared the programme with and would have concluded that he, and perhaps a few others, were amongst those that were almost certainly doomed. Hence, I believe, that forlorn statistic, as a means of giving us notice that he was not going to make it.

One night some months later, he is standing in our kitchen, deep in the throes of drink, staggering, unshaven, with the red face of the alcoholic who has been on a binge for days. We are just in the door from Bath in the south of England, where Rachel his sister has been directing Strindberg's *Miss Julie* for the Peter Hall Company at the Theatre Royal. It has been a triumph: four star reviews in *The Guardian* and *The Times*, Rachel being hailed as a great new director. The Donegal playwright Frank McGuinness, who made the translation from Strindberg, is overjoyed, as is Sir Peter Hall. She has transposed the play to a Northern Ireland setting, with electrifying results.

We come back to find Egan out of his skull. The kitchen is a mess, food all over the floor, drink spilt everywhere, the cat litter-tray unemptied, all the worktop surfaces covered in half-eaten debris and slops. I start to clean up as Egan is stumbling around in a dressing gown, filthy from days of abandon. Why does he do this nearly every time we are away? He is annoyed at my cleaning up, as he always is. I suppose I am not too good at hiding my anger and dismay. 'You're always cleaning,' he says. I suppose I am. It is often what I have no choice but to do for him.

He goes upstairs to try to tidy himself up; he has a shower, helped by his mother, for whom these situations are a kind of death. As she endures them, she goes completely silent, avoids any recrimination, knowing that the situation is like a forest floor after years of drought: one wrong word and the whole thing will flare up, and we shall all be engulfed by flames of rage and sorrow. I too have, on the whole, learned to keep my mouth shut.

Egan comes back down, looking slightly better and fills the kettle to make coffee. He has put some clothes on and is standing there in the kitchen, the electric light shining on his shaven head. He is swaying, still drunk. Beneath the stubble on his skull, I see that the eczema has come back again, and I experience an internal caving-in of hopeless pity.

Then he turns to me. He has been staring at the kettle that is starting to come to the boil, supporting himself with his two hands outstretched on the wooden worktop, and he turns and looks at me with his unfocused eyes and says: 'I can't stop; I won't ever be able to stop. I can't help it.' And he starts to cry. I go up to him and put my hands on his unshaven cheeks. I am crying now as well.

As I look at his suffering face, I have the feeling, one I have had many times before, that I am looking at a bodily realisation of the way things are with us now in the world. He is taking into his exhausted and abused body all the ills and toxins of what we are doing to each other, and what we are doing is so abominable now that we do not notice it any longer, so far gone are we in our blind indifference and thoughtless self-annihilation. Heidegger saw it in the 1930s, Beckett saw it in the 1950s and 1960s, and there are still some few who see it, among them the writers Geoffrey Hill, Doris Lessing and Cormac McCarthy. But generally it is the case that we are not alive to the condition we are in, to how bad it is. Egan is literally imbibing the poison of what we are, putrefying himself with it, craving it all the more, even as the damage it does to him destroys him.

I take my hands from his face and put my arms around him, feeling the thin bony body, the frail shoulders, the immense and racking pain and all I can say is: 'You poor man, you poor man. God help you.'

19

A Last Supper

The first Wednesday after Egan was admitted to St John of God's was the first of the weekly family days. Julie was longing to see him, so it was decided that she and I would make the first visit. She was scarcely able to contain her excitement and chattered all the way down during the four-hour drive. When we arrived, Egan was happy to see us. He greeted us, then brought us into the reception room where we had coffee and met the other family visitors. It was only a few days since he had been admitted but he looked magnificent. All his energy was back, his eyes were clear, and he was relaxed and easy in himself. Those remarkable powers of recovery that he had were underway.

The alcoholic patients who were admitted in the same week as Egan shared the same group. All were in their first week of treatment, so the visitors were sharing the first of their engagements with the process. After coffee and chat there was a general session in a large meeting room where everyone sat in chairs ranged around the walls. I was alarmed. We, the visitors, were meant to say how we felt about what living with an alcoholic meant to us, and to talk about what it did to our lives. The patients were to listen to this and not make any attempt to respond.

Some of the visitors spoke easily and openly about how they felt, the love they had for the person afflicted, the hurt they experienced, the disappointments, the anger. Others, me amongst them, found it appallingly difficult to say anything at all about such things. Some people, I have no doubt, spoke sincerely; but there were others who, it seemed to me, found this altogether too easy. A few made a meal of the whole thing. Declarations of love were forthcoming which sounded to me to be too formulaic to be convincing and these were, in a number of instances, mixed in with harsh recriminations and even ultimata masked as concern. What a bag of tricks the human heart is.

Julie entered into the spirit of the thing. She talked away about love and pain, and how hurt she was by Egan thinking only of himself. She talked volubly and without embarrassment, but this is part of the condition for which she was being treated in the Ross Thomson Unit: she has no instinct for self-censorship. A radical innocent, she speaks as she feels. I have seen her reduce pompous consultants to cowed silence. From time to time as she spoke, I looked at Egan's face, which had assumed a sphinx-like fixity. He was finding this hard.

I was relieved when it was time for lunch. The food was good and we ate well, Egan saying that it was generally up to this standard. It was a sunny day and the light gleamed on the cutlery and in the sparkling water we bought to accompany the food. I asked Egan if there was anything I could get him and he said that he could do with some fruit, so I went out, leaving him and Julie together. I crossed the busy main road to a shopping centre where there was, I noticed, a pub and off-licence (where in Ireland would there not be such within easy reach?). Could these places and the solace they bring be forever off-limits to Egan? Impossible, and yet I was hoping it might be so. Perhaps, I thought, as I walked back along the road walled in grey limestone, I could persuade him to go to Baroda in India where my friend and ex-student Ganesh Devy runs the Adivasi Academy. Ganesh's Academy is devoted to improving the lives of the nomadic tribes of India and accepts volunteers from all over the world, many of them wounded people looking for a new direction. Ganesh, a brilliant scholar, who left academic life to work with the adivasi, the so-called 'denotified' peoples, people of no account in Indian society, suggested such a course of action when I told him of Egan's suffering. He had known Egan as a little boy, had foretold that he would be wealthy, had bought him many ice-creams in Morelli's in Portstewart. 'Send him to me,' he said. 'He can work for us and teach computing. We will look after him; he will recover. Also, Gujurat is a dry state. He will not find it easy to get drink.' It was not to be.

After lunch there was a further session where the patients talked to their visitors while counsellors moved between what were now family meetings, most of them one-on-one. Again, we were expected to tell the alcoholic how we felt about their addiction and once more I found this very difficult. I said how sorry we were for Egan, that we cared for him, that it was awful when he was out of control. But nothing I could say connected to anything real. It was all just words. I felt like a washout, another term from Beckett's lexicon of misery.

Egan too found this session excruciating, but overall it was evident he was doing well. We met the friends he had made: a car mechanic from County Kildare, an estate agent from Wexford, a rich American girl suffering from anorexia as well as being alcoholic (her father had flown in from New York to be there and had said, resignedly, that this time he just hoped it would work), a brilliantly vivacious English girl (I noticed Julie keeping an eye on her). All generous and open people, all drawn to Egan, as so many were, for his candour, his transparency.

When we were leaving, Egan came out to the door to say good-bye. He embraced me, then Julie. I thought how forlorn it is for him to be left there in his affliction, while we headed off, able to stop anywhere we want, have a drink. His fate was to go through what he had to go through in there and (I know he was thinking this) was it worth it? He smiled at us and waved goodbye, standing in front of the big plate glass doors, smoking a cigarette. We walked to the car park, looking back all the time, waving.

Angela took over the remaining family sessions, greatly to my relief and, I am sure, Egan's also. Angela's presence is invariably a less burdensome one than mine, and that is because she carries her burdens lightly.

On 7 April 2006 Egan was discharged from St John of God's. We had discussed on the phone how he would travel back. My university responsibilities made it impossible for me to drive to Dublin: what I would give now to have those few hours with him that I let slip away through my futile sense of duty. In any case Egan was adamant that he wanted to get back under his own steam. This was a good sign. He had suffered panic attacks on public transport from about the age of fifteen, during his struggle with anorexia. Now here he was saying that he would make his own way back by train, and he had been on buses in Dublin. He and one of his friends at the hospital went into the centre of Dublin one Sunday (a day when many of the patients, most of whom lived within easy reach, went home) by bus, and had a day round the shops, which they finished off with an Italian meal, without drink (or so he said).

'No need to fetch me,' he said, 'I'll take the train and change at Belfast for Coleraine.' In the end it was agreed that I would collect him from Belfast Central. The plan was for him to stay with us for a few days before returning to the flat in Ballymoney.

Egan looked fit and healthy as he came through the gates from the platform. It was a crowded train, full of people coming north for the weekend, or returning from work in Dublin. Egan had a lot of bags, including his guitar. Arriving late at Connolly Station in Dublin, he found it impossible to get a seat in standard class, so he decided to travel in first. In the carriage was someone he knew, Bernie Hannigan, one-time Dean of Science at the university. She and I were friends. She did not see Egan on the train, though she knew him well, he having worked for her when he was involved in setting up the virtual school of biomedical sciences at Coleraine. He did see her, however, and what he saw was her ordering a gin and tonic from the waiter. Imagine Egan's state of mind. It is Friday evening; it is first class; he can order a drink; what harm could it do? Look at Bernie. Why can't he be just like her and have a drink? He orders a gin and tonic. Imagine the taste of this after four weeks of abstinence, the fizz of the tonic, the astringency of the lemon, the sweet musky juniper flavour of the gin. Imagine the pleasure of this, and then the terror and the remorse. Your parents have just spent £9,000 on treatment to help you stop drinking; the money is your inheritance, or that bit of it meant to get you started, and here you are failing at the first fence. It was months later before he confessed to us that his resolve broke down at the first trial.

As he walked towards me, he was looking rested and alert. Bernie was a few yards ahead of him. When I greeted her, he said hallo to her as well, all effusive friendliness, pretending not to have seen her. I embraced him as Bernie walked on. There was no smell of drink, but then it was the last thing I was looking for. I now know that this period, immediately after discharge from an alcohol treatment centre, is recognised as being an extremely dangerous one and it is vital that drinkers not be left on their own. They did not tell us this at St John of God's, but I should have figured it out for myself.

As I drove back to Coleraine, I asked him about the programme but he was not forthcoming. He was probably scared at the prospect of what faced him now, on his own with his addiction, without support. Alcoholics Anonymous holds that it is not possible for the addict to give up alcohol on his or her own. Some higher power is needed. This is one of the famous twelve steps, where the alcoholic admits that he or she is powerless over alcohol and that only a higher power can 'restore sanity'. Egan could not make that admission, could not accept the higher power, so he was on his own. In the deepest depths of his agony he was, I think, closer to Christ on the cross than many who proclaim the efficacy of a higher power. He did try AA a number of times, but the meetings were not for him. For a start, he found it hard to take all the talk about drink; he used to say that after an AA meeting he always felt the same way, that he would give anything for a drink. And, then he found it hard to credit people when they talked confidently of the higher power, as if, he would say, they were trying to convince themselves it was all true.

Christ on the cross is on his own; my God, my God, he shouts, why have you forsaken me? This desolation is what is at the heart of faith, not the cosy presumption that the higher power is a kind of supergas that you can fill up with at a convenient God station. The path of the true cross was the one Egan was destined to follow, the path of utter solitude, leading to the same place Christ entered in his last moments. If only my son could have come to value the solace the fellowship of AA can bring, but it was not to be. The programme at St John of God's, like almost all such programmes, is based on the twelve steps. To some extent, therefore, there would always have been, at the back of Egan's mind, a reservation about the method. That did not stop him from entering fully into the programme: his main counsellor told us that she had never seen anyone give himself so totally to the programme as Egan had. He really tried.

During the following days Egan was moody and troubled. Understandable enough, I thought. Julie was around quite a bit and her need to get assurance from him was demanding. Angela and I, too, were a pressure on him, observing his moods as he settled back into life outside the protective cocoon of the institution. Three people were looking at him, wondering what was to come next.

This tension continued until the Thursday following the Friday when he left the hospital, the Holy Thursday before Easter. It was about half past six in the evening when the explosion happened. I was upstairs, watching TV. Egan and his mother were downstairs, cooking. Then, suddenly, out of nowhere, there was an almighty crash of glass shattering followed by Egan's screams and shouts. I was stricken with fear. What was going on? I got to the door of the upstairs living room and I heard Angela shouting: 'Stop, stop.' More crashes, more smashing of glass. I tore downstairs, terrified.

Egan was very drunk and had gone berserk. Angela and I had, slightly earlier, gone out to the supermarket to get a few items for the meal he was cooking. We were out no more than half an hour. When we left, he was fine, but in that short space of time he had drunk himself into a frenzy. He tried to contain it and hid it from his mother for a while, but then, as he was turning with a saucepan, he staggered and spilled some of its contents. She asked him if he was OK. He growled that he was; then she asked him, full of fear, if he had been drinking and he went crazy, firing the saucepan at the wall, and smashing the two panels of frosted glass in the kitchen door. He slammed through that door out into the hallway and, with his bare fists, started breaking the picture frames and the glass in them which were hanging on the wall. He made for the stained glass in the inner door to the porch inside the front door and put his fists through these panels also. All this took place in seconds. I got down to the hallway as he was punching through the stained glass, but by now the damage had been done.

I pulled him back as he continued to drive his fists through the panels in the door. Shards of glass were sticking up from the leaded retainers, some still stuck in the frame. His hands were covered in blood, and there was blood all over the floor and walls. I dragged him away from the door, but he tried to push past me to get to the panels again. All the time he was screaming, me yelling back at him to try to get him to see sense. I stopped him but, as we struggled, he fell to the floor. He roars at me that he has never been prouder of me than now, now that I have pushed him down. He gets up and starts shouting at me to hit him. I say: 'No, I won't do that.' Again he begs me to hit him. I cannot. There is no anger in me, just sorrow. A few times before, in drink, he has asked me to hit him. I have never been able to do it, but he has wanted me to, in some obscure desire for punishment.

After a few minutes he calms down, and Angela and I bring him back into the kitchen, sit him down and clean him up as best we can. He is shaking with shock and adrenalin. He is badly cut all over his hands and arms. I clear up the shattered glass from the kitchen and hallway floors and wipe my son's blood from the floor, walls, the stair handrail and spindles. As I brush up the glass, there is the sickening silvery sound of the shards scraping against themselves.

Angela thinks we should call Ian McNie. I agree. There has not ever been anything like this and it seems right to have someone else there, someone with Ian's gentle authority. He immediately agrees to come over from Ballymoney and suggests he bring with him John McConaghey, a parish worker, and someone who has been kind to Egan. John is a tall, strong man, and there may have been a precautionary element in Ian asking him along, just in case.

When they come in, Ian glances at the damage and looks at me in anguish. John and he are both pale and quiet. Egan is sitting in the kitchen, woozy now, bandaged. As well as the cuts to his arms and hands, he has a gash on his back where he fell back onto a piece of glass when I pushed him down. I make tea. We have eaten nothing, because the meal Egan was cooking ended up on the floor and walls, so I suggest I go out and get fish and chips for all of us. I return in a half an hour or less, unwrap the food and put it out on plates, with vinegar and brown and red sauce. We have tea and bread and butter with it, a meal from my childhood. We eat, ravenously; we are all hungry, believe it or not. Ian asks Egan why he did it. He cannot say. He is sorry, so sorry he says. 'I will,' he says, 'pay for the damage.' He knows how much I liked the stained glass in the inner door of the porch. They were Victorian originals, which I had discovered set into a crude frame in the bare brick wall of the loft to our garage. They had been taken out of the porch door and replaced by plain frosted glass to let in more light, probably in the 1960s.

Egan also said, that night, that he would pay us back the cost of his treatment at St John of God's. With what? At this time and when he died there was a court action relating to a business matter which, he believed (and legal advice supported his view), would go in his favour. Such an outcome would result in a significant settlement, which meant that Egan always entertained the idea that serious money was in the offing. This prospect was a factor in his drinking. As is usual in such cases, there were long delays, which meant that his life was on hold, as he waited, and the agony of waiting is a good excuse to drink. Furthermore, the expected money gave him an illusory sense of security, so that made it OK to drink. There you have two good excuses to imbibe: the stress of waiting; the likelihood of a 'sure thing'.

Alcoholics will always find excuses. One of Egan's fellow patients at St John of God's was someone who had been a senior civil servant. He lost a leg in an accident and during recovery started to drink. He was married, the marriage was childless, and then, while still recovering from the amputation, his wife suddenly died. When he recounted this dreadful story to the group in one of their internal sessions, the counsellor said: 'Well now, didn't that give you a brilliant excuse to drink?' Harsh but searingly accurate.

Ian felt that Egan should be admitted to hospital (he had been out of St John of God's for less than a week), not so much because of his cuts, but because he could do with being kept under observation, and assessed once again for admission to the Ross Thomson

Unit. I said that I did not think he would be admitted. It was the same old problem, in my opinion. The view in the hospital would be that he would have to deal with the alcohol problem before they could begin to treat him, whereas the alcohol abuse was itself a symptom of whatever it was that was troubling him deep down.

'I don't know,' said Ian. 'I think he should be in hospital.' He took control, making calls to nurses, doctors, consultants, letting them know who he was, minister of Trinity Presbyterian. These credentials worked wonders. His calm persuasiveness was listened to, and doors opened. As if by magic (or the grace of God), Egan was admitted that night to the Ross Thomson Unit. He was once more in safe hands.

To this day there is still a drop of dried blood from that night on the frame above the door that leads from the hallway into my study, a drop that must have flown up during the mayhem and the struggle. I missed it that night when I cleaned up the streaks and puddles of blood on the floor and walls. I have left it there and will never clean it off. It is a memory of my dead son, a fragment, now dried and lifeless, of his living blood that he wanted, so badly, to shed. And that he wanted me to draw. Why? To be punished for what he had done, for letting us down? Partly that. There was his suicide message of November later that year, written in the notebook he intended to give me as a Christmas present, where he said that he hated hurting us. So, yes, I think he wanted to be punished for hurting us and asked me, many times, to hit him hard.

Something in Egan craved punishment, but it was not just in retribution for wrongs done to those he loved and who loved him. There was this 'something else' he referred to in the suicide note of November 2006. It was this something else that eventually killed him. I connect this to what the Gospels reveal about the meaning of suffering. A person's death, considered in the usual way – the factual way, is just that: a blunt fact, a dreary inevitability that points to the futility of our strutting banality and arrogance. But a certain kind of suffering, a certain kind of death is possible, which removes death from its finality, its terminal absoluteness. This kind of death becomes the means, the form, through which 'something else' takes place.

A certain kind of suffering, a certain kind of death which follows it, puts itself in the way of becoming not a thing in itself, with terminal finality, but a moving onwards, a reissuing, a change, a new surge of being, a resurrection. It becomes 'something else'. This, I believe, was the meaning of Egan's suffering that Holy Thursday, and the reason for the brooding of the days before. He was putting himself into the way of being the form through which suffering becomes 'something else', something for others, for you, in the words of the consecration. He was putting himself into the way of the cross.

It was a dreadful (that is, full of dread) choice he made when he took the drink on the way back home in the train from Dublin. He was, in that moment, choosing suffering and death with, I am certain, a clear interior instinct about the nature of what it was he was embarking upon, the way of death. That delicious and ravishing sip of gin and tonic as the train thundered north past Rush and Julianstown and Bettystown towards his destiny was the moment in which he decided, once and for all, to begin to have a death-oriented way of being. That means a way that looked to the cross and resurrection. In death only is there the resurrection. One begets the other.

That Holy Thursday night, after the howling distress, the violence, the blood, the broken glass, the torn skin, the visit of the two apostles from Ballymoney, little did I know that the supper I went out to buy, the supper of fish and chips, was a kind of Last Supper, a faint recall of the Last Supper of the first Holy Thursday. Nor that the blood that was shed was the blood of a lamb, of our son Egan, who was shedding his blood for us in the way of suffering he had chosen, the blood that still daubs the door of my study where I am now writing this.

The Last Supper in the New Testament is a creation of a 'new and everlasting covenant' between man and God. Christ is the lamb that is to be sacrificed, and the first Eucharist that is the Last Supper is a deliberate recalling of the sacrificial lamb of the Passover. In Exodus, the Israelites are in captivity in Egypt. God sends ten plagues on the Egyptians to force the Pharaoh to release the Jews and the last of these is the death of all first-born sons in the land of Egypt.

God tells Moses to instruct the Israelites to sacrifice a lamb for every household. The blood of the lamb must be daubed on the doorposts and lintels of their homes so that when the angel of death comes, he will see the blood sign and pass over: 'And the blood shall be to you for a token upon the houses where ye are: and when I see the blood, I will pass over you, and the plague shall not be upon you to destroy you, when I smite the land of Egypt.'

Egan's blood will stay on my doorframe for as long as I live in this house. It is the sign of a new covenant, of the forgiveness of sins. My sins. All of them.

20

Mute

Egan is gone. It is now May 2008 and I am writing during a day of warm spring sunshine under a willow that he once pruned and shaped. He knew, by instinct, to place a supporting strut under the sagging trunk to straighten it back into true, the tree having sunk down too far under its own weight. It remained upright when he took the support away. He got the pruning just right, lightening the burden for the tree, so it could lift up its branches once more into the air and light. Parsnipia, his cat, walks past me to check out the hunting possibilities up the back garden. She is a lithe, beautiful and deadly creature: she regularly murders birds and consumes every morsel of them, apart from the feathers, which she leaves strewn about the grass in a circle, as if to say to us – look what I can do. I have seen her jump five feet into the air from prone position to catch a butterfly in her mouth. It would be like a man jumping, from standing, the height of a house. Egan adored this cat which Julie found for him in Ballymoney; the best present ever, he said, when she brought her to him. The poor thing lived through his drunken times in the flat in John Street, puzzled and terrified by the change in the creature who loved her, whom she loved, a creature who, one day would take her in his arms and hold her, and on another might walk on top of her without meaning to.

Egan was missing from 28 January, the Sunday. His twenty-seventh birthday was to have fallen on the following Wednesday.

During this time, Angela went round to his house on Brook Street to feed the cat and look after her. Parsnipia would sit in the front window looking out, waiting for him, pacing the narrow white sill between the rattling blinds and the glass.

The police investigation and the search went on over these days. One large constable, laden with the accoutrements of his trade, all slung round a huge leather belt (gun, crackling intercom, truncheon, handcuffs, hand-held computer), insisted on searching the house from the attic at the top to the garage and its loft. He even went up the small ladder that connects the attic to the roof space under the slates. This is in fact one of the hallowed and haunted places. It was where Angela once found him when she got back from work. It was after five. She called out, nervous, as always, as to what she might find. He now did not ever want to leave the house and he would spend the day there, drinking, phoning cronies (such as he still had) or taxi drivers, to go to the off-licence and get his drink. Angela was worried that he might choke on his vomit; or that he would set fire to himself, as happened to two alcoholics we knew of in the Triangle area. She became agitated when there was no reply and started to search the house. He was not in his bedroom, nor was he anywhere downstairs, or watching TV, or playing on the Xbox, which he had bought in a sober phase to try to distract himself from his cravings. She went up to the attic. No sign. And then she climbed up the little ladder into the roof space, the final option, and there he was, cowering in the farthest corner, in the dark, head down on his knees, shaking and crying.

'What's the matter?' she asked. 'I'm frightened,' he said. 'Of what?' 'Of what Dad will say.' 'He won't say anything, he'll just be glad you're alright.' 'No,' he said, 'he'll be mad at me for being so weak that I can't stop drinking.'

I would not be mad at him. I would be sorry. Anger was something that had effectively left me at this stage, or at least when it came to anything to do with my poor son. I tended to reserve it for the whining pusillanimity of my academic colleagues, their puny arrogance and self-concern. But even there, Egan's suffering had taught me more restraint and control. What did most of them know about the brutal actualities from which Egan had learned good manners and decorum? To most of them, fate had not shown the vicious and tangled threads below her fanged smile. Or at least not yet. She will always put in an appearance, in every life, but for many in the comfort zones of academe, those visits tend to come at the end, when ease recedes and the academics begin to realise, to their horror, how blind they have been to the frantic shears of life, how right the ancient Greek tragedians were.

The police search observed the necessary routine. Beginning at Brook Street, they moved out from there, interviewing householders, searching garages and sheds, taking our house into the net as it widened. That was when the big constable with the weight of equipment went up to the roof-space and came down the three flights of stairs panting from his exertions, so that he had to sit down when he came to the kitchen. So encumbered was he with his gadgets that he could not fit into a chair in the kitchen with armrests. It is ridiculous what you notice in the unreality of never-remitting tension.

A helicopter flew up and down the river searching its banks. It even did a search at night when there was a low tide. Taxi drivers were questioned, as were the staff in the bars in the town. No evidence was found, no reports of Egan's whereabouts turned up. He had, in fact, we learned later, been in a bar, the Clyde on Railway Road, but somehow it failed to emerge that the barmaid questioned there was not working on the Saturday he went missing and that someone else was.

And then, on Thursday, 1 February, the first day of Angela's dreaded month, the day after Egan's birthday, news came that a shoe had been found on the riverbank at a place called the Loughan, an ancient ford of the Bann. Paul Meikle, the police liaison officer assigned to the case, called to ask if he could come round with the shoe to see if Angela was able to identify it. As it happened, Charlotte was also in the house. While they waited for Paul Meikle Charlotte paced the kitchen floor repeating, 'please don't let it be Egan's, please don't let it be Egan's', like a mantra. The shoe was in fact Egan's. Angela had been with him a week or two before when he had bought the shoes at a store called Petroleum in Coleraine. She recalled how pleased he had been, because the shoes, half trainers, half normal shoe design, were brilliant but inexpensive copies of some exclusive make.

Paul Meikle requested an underwater search team. The nearest available unit was in Yorkshire and they were engaged until the beginning of the following week. They arrived on the Monday and started their searches the next day. All this time, to the surprise of many, Angela and I continued to go to work. It was better than hanging around waiting for news when no news would, we knew, be forthcoming. I was now certain that the river had taken our son.

On the Wednesday I had a long-standing invitation to deliver, at Queen's University in Belfast, a talk as part of their extramural literature series known as the Edith Devlin lectures, named after the immensely popular person who had given most of them over the previous twenty years or so. Recently, she has taken to inviting in the occasional guest lecturer, and I was to be one of these. My subject was, ironically enough, given what we were going through in those days, to be the so-called 'Locus Amoenus', the pleasant or delightful place, a dominant theme in literature and painting since writing and visual art began, which means, really, since the beginning of the human species on this earth. To be human is to dream of the amenable place, the bower, the grove, the secret garden, where we can get away for a while from what Yeats called the 'fury and the mire of human veins'.

When I arrive at Queen's to give the lecture, I am agitated and clogged by the fury and the mire that runs through human veins. Parking has been arranged for me by an old friend and poet, Tess McGuiness, who helps Edith Devlin run the lectures, and I find a space behind the red-bricked Whitla Hall. Near the parking bays is a row of dustbins to take the refuse from the kitchens nearby. I get my car, an old and hefty Jaguar, into one of the confined spaces and squeeze out the door which is right up against the next vehicle. There is, behind me, the sound of a raven croaking and cawing. When I can turn round to look, I see a large black bird standing on a low brick wall no more than four feet from the rear of the car. I move towards it but it does not fly away. It hops from foot to foot, cawing and snorting, jerking its long beak up and down and ruffling its feathers. Raising its wings and extending them, it alights to the ground where it scrabbles with its claws and beak at an empty crisp bag, looking up at me from time to time. This goes on for two or three minutes, and I have the unmistakable feeling that the creature is trying to communicate with me. Something is trying to get through.

As I looked at the frantic urgency of the raven, whose head and yellow eyes kept swivelling in my direction, I was certain, beyond any doubt, that this was a message from Egan to let me know that things were OK. I have since learned, from a folklorist I met in Milan at a symposium on the writer Michele Spina (whom I knew in Leeds, and who became Egan's godfather), that the raven in folklore is recognised as the emissary of the dead. And this is not just the case in Ireland, the scholar Catherine O'Byrne from California told me; the native Americans of the west coast also believe that the raven carries messages from the dead to the living.

I say goodbye to the raven under my breath, leaving it to its wrestle with the crisp bag, and walk over to the lecture theatre, thinking of the realm of the dead, the great unknown. Those who try to make contact with that world perhaps only usurp its proper quiet. There was ever only one person who had the power to bring back the dead to life; or at least that is what I believe and put my trust in, my hope. Those who practice as spiritualists are not, for the most part, out to deceive. Human life and emotion being so intense, people being loved so much and loving so much in return, it is surely, more often than not, an impulse of kindness, rather than a trick of exploitation, to maintain that it is possible to make contact with those who have 'gone before'. Surely, they feel, it cannot be right that those we love disappear without a trace. And if there is a trace, then contact must be possible. Are there not ghosts? Is not contact made with something when people conjure with a glass or a Ouija board? (In fact, my Sardinian friend Pino Serpillo is quite certain that he has had a number of contacts from the dead, on one occasion testing the spirit's statements against actual circumstance.)

These are difficult and awkward issues. What we can be sure of is this: for millennia, for as long as there has been a human species, there has been an absolute conviction that the dead are not just no more; at the same time we acknowledge that there is a deep and mysterious gulf between whatever their realm is, and that of the living. Across this abyss it is profoundly difficult, and perhaps impossible, to transmit messages. The labyrinth at Knossos on Crete, the pyramids of Egypt, the Mayan burial rites and mausolea, all give strong indications along the following lines: that those who are living are everywhere driven to create structures to bury their dead; that these structures embody the awe of the living at the baffling silence that obtains between them and those who have 'gone before'; that these structures, the funerary monuments, register in their grim and enigmatic magnificence the contrast between those whose brains, tongues and limbs still function, and those for whom these functions no longer obtain, or at least not in ways that are familiar to us. And yet, it is also the case that for millennia there has existed a certainty that something sometimes does get across. Hence my curious exhilaration that the croaking raven was trying to tell me something as I got out of the car behind the Whitla Hall, even as the Yorkshire divers were searching the swollen waters of the Bann for the body of my son.

Rachel, Egan's sister, was stricken by her brother's death. A few days after he went missing she had a strange experience. It was night. She was in bed in her house in Belfast, where Egan had stayed many times, and the kitchen of which he and Steve Kirk (Welch and Kirk Developments) had fitted out in rustic style. She woke up as someone was tickling her feet, the kind of thing, she says, Egan would do. It was not completely dark, and she could see there was no one there. She was not asleep, she was not dreaming, and she was not scared. Someone's finger was scratching the soles of her feet, one by one. Then a presence, which she knew to be Egan she says, got into bed beside her, the mattress sinking down beneath this new weight. She felt it dip away from her. A deep sensation of comfort descended. Egan had come, she says, to let her know he was at peace.

I met up with Tess McGuiness and we went along to the lecture theatre. There are over two hundred people, mostly middle-aged or elderly, in the large hall. This is the kind of audience the famous Edith Devlin lectures attract. I start on my topic, the Locus Amoenus, the opposite to where my son, I am sure, lies in the cold waters of the Bann. I quote the *Eclogues* of Virgil, the great Latin poem about the seasonal rhythms and harmony of nature, with its restful places that give solace to the spirit. I discuss Edmund Spenser's evocations of idealised Irish landscapes in *The Faerie Queene* and *Prothalamion*, after the poem celebrating his marriage in Cork to Elizabeth Boyle. I then move on to Wordsworth, to his *Poems of the Imagination* (1800), and the piece called 'There was a Boy'.

I am unprepared for what happens next. I start reading the words and cannot get beyond the opening phrases: 'There was a Boy; ye knew him well, ye Cliffs/ And Islands of Winander'. I have to stop. Poetry can do this to you. The emotional charge in the words is sometimes so strong that if you are to any extent vulnerable to onrushes of feeling, then the language can communicate the intensity in which the poem was originally conceived; the whole thing gets reborn. The writer, if he or she is about his business correctly, feels everything. This is what the novelist Colm Tóibín said to Angela and to me one morning as we were having coffee in Charlottesville, Virginia. Very simple, very true. This 'feeling everything', this maximised sensitivity, gets into the words, and poetry is the form language takes when it goes for the whole thing. So that poetry, because it is poetry, and therefore language at its extreme pitch of intensity, will have a heightened charge of energy that recreates the original feeling. All Wordsworth's feelings for the dead boy rise up again in the language as I read it from the lectern. His feeling for this nameless child who died in Windermere is mixed up with my own terrible emotion about my son; and the language releases this potent amalgam. I hate it when this kind of thing happens to me, as it does from time to time. I stop and ask Tess to read the poem, which she does, very well. I then comment on what Wordsworth is doing. He has created this beautiful place, where the boy lived and now death enters. The poem ends like this:

> Pre-eminent is the vale
> Where he was born and bred: the churchyard hangs
> Upon a slope above the village-school;
> And through that churchyard where my way has led

On summer evenings, I believe that there
A long half-hour together I have stood
Mute – looking at the grave wherein he lies!

These are some of the greatest and simplest lines in English poetry, itself probably the greatest poetic tradition the world has known.

I wanted to show the audience the artistry involved in this power. I drew attention to the word 'Mute'. I asked them to observe how it was positioned, how it arrives, at the head of the line, with a sudden shock and force after the verb that ends the previous line, 'stood'. An adverb telling us more about the verb it relates to, that he stood 'mute', it holds up the flow of the line, and lets a mute silence enter. The word is followed by a dash; there is meant to be a silence in the flow of language to draw attention to the gulf between the realms of the living, those who use language, who can stand by a grave and be, for a 'long half-hour together' silent, and those like the boy who are dead, who are beyond our language, whose whole realm is silence. Mute, there is nothing to be said. When we meet someone who has been bereaved we say (as many said to us): 'What can I say? No words will do. I am sorry.' Wordsworth has put that very inadequacy into the masterly words of his great poem, in which silence is so eloquently deployed. Death enters the poem.

Meanwhile the divers from Yorkshire are searching the river. The Bann is in spate. There has been so much rainfall in recent weeks that the water is silted and muddy, the visibility underwater very poor. The divers can see no more than a foot in front of their faces, so the search is conducted by touch as they grope along the river-bed. They dive again and again all Tuesday and Wednesday and find nothing. They are searching close to the spot where the shoe was found. A marina, where water skis and power-boats can be hired, fronts the river. Set back from the bank are some wooden chalets, which are rented out to holidaymakers in the summer and to students and others in the winter. A gravel expanse stretches between the chalets and the water, above which float a couple of wooden jetties with moorings and bollards for boats. The shoe was found on a grassy verge above the river. At this point the bank slopes steeply and there is no jetty. It would be easy to fall in here, in the dead of night, especially if you were drunk or confused.

We are told that if the body is not found soon the police search will have to be abandoned; at that point we can bring in our own divers if we wish, but not before, because there are protocols governing these duties. We know that some bodies are never found: a few years ago three fishermen on the Bann disappeared; their overturned boat was recovered but they vanished without trace. Sometimes people who drown in the Bann are swept out to sea and their bodies can turn up, weeks later, off the Mull of Kintyre in Scotland, or on some Hebridean shore.

The next day, Thursday, I am at work as usual when the call comes. I am, in fact, trying to sort out a disagreement between two senior members of the Faculty, a collision between arrogance on the one hand and a (to my mind perfectly reasonable) refusal to yield to emotional bullying and deliberate obfuscation. There are the usual useless squads of angry accusations being released by the bully, who knows also how to get upset strategically so as to cloud the issue, when what is afoot is an egotistical and malicious determination to undermine the other person. In other words, I am helplessly embroiled in a typically mindless academic squabble raised by a troublemaker, where the emotional investment, which is immense, is in inverse proportion to the importance of the issue. When the call comes from Paul Meikle, I excuse myself from this vexatiousness and go outside to speak to him. Paul gravely tells me that the divers have found the body of a young man. They first located an orange-coloured scarf on the riverbed and then, a few feet away, a corpse. The police are sure it is Egan, but they would like someone to identify the body. I do not have to do it, he says; they have other ways of verification, but it would be a help if I could bring myself to face it. 'Will you do it?' Paul asks, respectfully. I say yes.

I go back in and tell my colleagues, who are sitting in silence, what has happened and cannot refrain from saying that this should put their petty issues into perspective. They leave. I go into the office to tell Pearl, my secretary, what I have agreed to do. I tidy up a few things then go.

I drive back home where Angela and Charlotte are waiting in some wild arena of bafflement and fear. It is a fact, or it is shortly to be proved to be so, that Egan, our son, the man Charlotte has promised to marry, is dead. When I get to the Loughan, Paul is waiting for me. He tells me that Father Keaney, our parish priest, has been and that he has said the Last Rites over Egan. We had asked him to do this if the body were recovered and Paul has arranged it, contacting Father Keaney immediately. He was certain it was Egan. The identification was a formality. Paul, being a Catholic, was able to assist in the administration of the Rites, saying the responses.

Egan's body is lying on one of the wooden jetties. It is zipped up in a black body bag. Paul brings me down to it, through the police tape and past the knot of officers and wet-suited divers, who are packing up. I thank them. No problem, one of them says, and another says he is sorry for my trouble. I go down on to the slippery timber and come to the prone figure. Paul bends down and unzips the hood. There is my son's face, serene in death. His mouth is relaxed, his eyes closed. He has been in the water for eleven days. The skin is slightly darkened from the muddy river, but the overwhelming impression is of a face at peace. He is out of this 'rough world'. There is a contusion to his forehead, a darker stain. I tell Paul that this is Egan's body and he zips up the hood as I turn away. I take a few steps along the jetty, then go back and ask Paul to let me see him again. I will not see him ever again in this world. Paul unzips the hood once more and I bend down to touch his beloved face, his forehead, his cold cheek.

21

Upriver

Angela and I, on the last night Egan was alive, left his house at around half past five to go back to the retail park and buy an axe to chop the cherry tree that has been felled. Charlotte left, she told us, about six, maybe slightly before. She was going out, as were we. It was a Saturday night. Egan was left to himself. He said he would rent a few DVDs. God knows how lonely he felt that night.

He must have left the house immediately as Charlotte drove off to Portstewart because I later found out, reading the statements from the various people he was with that night, that he arrived at the Clyde Bar on Railway Road at about quarter past six. He had on a black overcoat and an orangey-red scarf, the colours of the otherworld he was now entering. In the Clyde he met someone he had known at school and that person's girlfriend. This young man asked him back to their house up in the Mountsandel area of the town, where the girlfriend cooked a meal for them and more drink was taken. Egan was now drinking through the Antabuse, as the footballer and alcoholic George Best used to do, with all the disastrous consequences that follow. If you drink on top of this powerful aversion drug, you develop extreme nausea, the heart rate drives up, the entire body starts to go into panic. Eventually Egan passed out on the sofa in their living room. After three in the morning, he came to, confused, drunk and sick. His hosts had gone to bed.

What happened from now on is not clear, and I have not tried too hard to find out exactly what took place, on the grounds that it is of no use to anyone to uncover all the sad and angry exchanges that will have gone on between a drunk and sick man who has become difficult and angry, and two people who have let themselves in for something far removed from what they would have expected. From the accounts I have had from the police and from what I have read, Egan seems to have gone crazy from the drink and medication, and become aggressive. He wanted to get home. He tried to call a taxi and failed. His friend called other taxi companies. At that hour, even on a Sunday morning, there would be few cabs running in Coleraine. Those that were out were booked solid. Egan became more and more objectionable and the girl insisted that he leave. The friend has been to sleep, but he knows he is still over the legal limit, so he cannot drive Egan home. Instead, he offers to drive him to the top of the housing development, to the main road, the Mountsandel Road. From there Egan may be able to flag down a cab, and, if not, it is only a twenty-minute walk home.

It is all somewhat obscure, but what seems to have happened is that Egan was indeed taken up to the main road, but instead of heading in towards town and his house, he heads off in the opposite direction, out into the country, towards the Loughan. The road he was now on was his final road.

He is heading upriver. He gets to the Loughan. Next to it is the marina with its chalets. There is a light on in one. He knocks. It is after four o'clock. By chance – it seems, by mischance – he has come upon a place where late-night drinking is in progress. He tells the man who answers the door that he is lost and asks if he can come in for a while. One of the three people inside recognises him and he is allowed in. Egan has, for a few years now, moved on the margins of the Coleraine underworld – the drinkers, addicts, drifters, pushers, petty criminals. He may even have hung around from time to time with street drinkers. He was drawn to this society, as Christ was. At any rate, the man who knows who Egan is, inside the chalet, is someone who frequented the open-air drinking haunts along the Bann by the old bridge. Egan is welcomed and given more to drink.

He passes out again. When he wakes up, an altercation develops and there is some unpleasantness. He is asked to leave. He appears to have accepted this quietly, as was usually his way, and he heads out into the pitch dark without protest. It is as if he always expects to be cast out of the light. It is his fate. He walks away from the chalet, the door now closed behind him. He probably thinks he is going to the entrance of the marina, which is to his left, when in fact he is walking straight towards the Bann.

He crossed the gravel and came to a rough pathway. This path is actually along the riverbank. Beside it there ran a length of black flex, connecting some makeshift lighting, strung along the bollards, to a power supply in the marina offices. All the lights were off. Egan seems to have stumbled, perhaps over the flex, and hit his head against an iron stanchion stuck in the riverbank as a mooring post, hence perhaps the contusion I saw on his forehead. He lost his footing, it seems, and as he did so one of his shoes came off. He then either slid or fell into the fast-flowing and icy waters of the Bann.

Paul Meikle thought that what I have outlined above is probably what happened, but of course there is no way we can know for certain what went on in those last few moments. Paul took away the stanchion to have it tested for traces of DNA. There were none. There was no suspicion of foul play. A death by misadventure was recorded some months later. No inquest was held, the coroner being satisfied by the police evidence and by the statements taken from those who had seen Egan in the hours before his death that no purpose would be served in instigating such a process. The coroner, who was unfailingly courteous and respectful, asked us if we wished to have the inquest in any case, but we agreed with him that there would be no point in such an undertaking. The reports that an inquest would generate would reawaken for us the terrible days and hours of waiting for news and would, also, damage Egan's dignity by making public the ignominy of aspects of his life and death.

We were given a taste of what that might be like. On the day after the body was recovered a major newspaper in Northern Ireland published a large photograph above a report of the recovery of the body. The photograph was taken from a boat on the water, or from the opposite bank with a telescopic lens. It showed the wooden jetty, the body bag, Father Keaney administering Extreme Unction and Paul Meikle. I protested to the newspaper and to the Press Complaints Commission that this was an invasion of privacy. The response I got was that it was not an infringement of this kind because a riverbank is a public arena and therefore not subject to the laws governing privacy. This was a disgusting episode, on a number of fronts: that such a photograph was taken by a photographer (I saw him, a well-known figure in the Coleraine area, hanging around the Loughan as soon as word was out that a search was on); that someone (whom I do not know) allowed it to be taken (this would have involved a boat or access to land on the far bank); that someone passed the word to the photographer when a body was found; and finally, after all this revolting intrusion, that a newspaper published the image.

22

Kicking the Black Mamba

The funeral was on 12 February. St John's chapel, on The Heights above Coleraine, looking down over the Bann, was packed. The aisles down the side of the church, the space at the back, the gallery upstairs, were thronged. Outside the main doors a great crowd of people stood in the open air. The family gathered: Angela's brother Flor and his wife Marian; my own sisters, Marian, Eileen and Teresa; Dominic, my brother.

When the service was over and the Mass for the Dead was said, Killian, Tiernan, Richard (our son-in-law) and I carried the coffin out on our shoulders, down the path leading to the grave. It began to rain. He was lowered in. Rachel stepped forward and tore from her neck a gold cross, which she threw into the grave on top of the coffin. It was not a theatrical gesture, it was one of hopeless love. Hundreds of people came up to sympathise. I embraced them all, including someone I had fallen out with years back. I forgave him, he forgave me, on the spot. Many wept when they held me. Among those paying their respects were the writers Alan Titley (who came all the way from Cork), Michael and Edna Longley, Patrick Ramsey, Damian Smyth and Ciaran Carson, the last in full mourning, long black coat, black hat. The hat was something, he told me (when I asked him later) he had found in a second-hand shop somewhere, a smallish thing with a narrow brim. It was dignified and proper, and gave Ciaran the look of someone from the early nineteenth century, a scholar arriving from the last survival of a Bardic School in some place like Corcomroe, in County Clare. I remember thinking this as I am standing at my son's grave. The mind is a whirlwind, as some Buddhist scripture says.

Tea and refreshments (and drink) are served in the town hall in the centre of Coleraine after the funeral. An old friend of mine (whom I will call Fintan) is there, wearing an incongruously bright yellow tie, because Egan gave it to him as a present when my friend was in hospital some months before. Fintan points to the tie and says: 'You'll know why I am wearing this. I'm wearing it for Egan.' 'Yes,' I say, 'I know'. The fact that this man has the character and wit to do this for Egan is one of the reasons why he and I are friends. Fintan had been very ill, close to death in fact, and Egan was not sure if he had been aware that a gift was made. This put Egan out a little, because he had, as ever, not spared himself when it came to the purchase, the tie being the most expensive he could buy. However, he was keen that Fintan should know how good it was, because its value was to be an indication of how great Egan's respect was for this man. He need not have worried. Fintan is a man who understands this kind of nuance perfectly.

Kicking the black mamba. It is what Egan did that Saturday night when, on his own, he walked into the Clyde Bar at quarter past six, intending, probably, to have no more than one drink. But as another alcoholic once said to me: 'One is too many, a hundred is not enough.'

Another friend of mine, a colleague at the university, was struggling with alcohol and was in danger of losing the battle. He stopped drinking on the advice of his doctors, and began quickly to improve in health, whereas his life was once in danger. He knew Egan and, during his fight to gain control of his addiction, Egan and he would talk, sometimes for hours at a time. Egan was insistent that this person was exactly at the point he had been at eighteen months before, and that our friend's illness would follow the same course unless he stopped drinking, something Egan feared he could not accomplish. He wrote as much in a long and carefully analytic letter to this man. As it happened, our friend has come through this difficult time, fully restored, his drinking (because he can take a drink) now under control. But this recovery came about only after Egan's death.

Some months before that day in January 2007, when Egan was lost to the waters of the Bann, he and I were discussing our friend, Egan pressing me as to whether or not this person was staying off the booze. I decided to tell him the truth and said to Egan that, yes, he was taking a drink again, but from what I could see he seemed to have it under control. 'He's what?' said Egan. 'He's drinking?' 'Yes,' I said, but he seems fine with it.' 'No,' said Egan, 'he's kicking the black mamba.' 'He's what?' I asked. Egan repeated the phrase, saying that was what this man was doing. He explained to me that the black mamba is one of the most venomous snakes on earth and a bite from it means almost certain death. Not only that, these snakes move very fast so, once they are roused, it is not easy to get away from them. I asked Egan where he got this saying from, thinking it was a quotation he had come across. 'I just made it up,' he said. 'It's what he's doing: he's kicking the black mamba that will kill him.'

23

Sophy's Dream

About a week after the funeral I had a letter from Sophy Hillen in Belfast, whose son John had become friends with Egan during their teens. At one time they had a band, rehearsals for which posed all kinds of problems: Egan and his brother Tiernan and the singer, a girl called Katie Andrew, were in Portstewart; John was in Belfast; and the drummer was from Ballycastle. The fathers of the various members spent hours driving around the province in cars, the back seats and boots of which were crammed with amps, bass drums, cymbals, keyboards. This is a common enough hazard of late-capitalist fatherhood, as offspring dream the dreams of fame. I have, however, never had anything like the experience of Andrew Hadfield, an ex-PhD student of mine, now professor of Renaissance literature at the University of Sussex. He was walking by his garage one afternoon where his son's band was practising and he heard, with a shock, the lyrics of the manic song they were roaring. The chorus went: 'I hate Dad'. That was his thanks, as he put it to me, for driving around Brighton with a cymbal jammed into the back of his neck.

John and Egan, when they were friends, were going through difficult times. Egan was anorexic, and John too had some emotional problems. But they were kind to each other and they seemed to have a lot to laugh about. They were handsome boys. Egan then had (the words will seem strange, but they are the right ones) an unearthly beauty; even I, his father, was struck by it. The anorexia had made him extraordinarily thin, emphasising his strong, high cheekbones, making his blue eyes bluer, aquamarine even. His then thick hair, worn long, fell over his pale strong jaw and high forehead. John was intense, deeply well-mannered, with light fair hair, hazel eyes, and slightly burnished skin. They spent hours together, talking about what boys of that age talk about, which is mostly, I think, about hope and possibility, rather than the vanities usually attributed to them.

Shocked by Egan's death, John was grief-stricken at the funeral, as was Sophy. The letter she sent contained remarkable things. In a dream she had, Egan, dazed and confused, is wandering in a grey, misty place when an older woman approaches him. She exudes kindness. On each side of her is a male figure. Stretching out her hand to him, she asks Egan if he will come with her. He is wary and shakes his head. He says: 'I don't know where this is; I don't know you.' She says: You know John, don't you?' 'Yes,' Egan says. Then, she says: 'This is John's uncle and his great-uncle.' The uncle, Sophy explains in the letter, is Seamus, her brother, who was killed in a car crash in 1987. The older man is Sophy's grand-uncle, John, a priest who died tragically young, aged twenty-nine, and after whom Egan's friend was named. The two men are happy and at peace and Egan feels he can trust them. Now Egan says: 'I want to see my Mum and Dad.' This is exactly what he would do and say. But the woman says: 'You will have to get well first because you aren't ready to see anybody just yet. We'll take you to a place where you will be healed.' Then he goes with them very trustingly, like a child, Sophy wrote. They leave the grey foggy place and move up a grassy, open, sunlit hill, on top of which is a building bathed in light. Egan is to go in here. Before he leaves, he tells Sophy that he wanted to send us something at the funeral; he wanted to send us light. And indeed, as Sophy reminds Angela and me in the letter, at the end of the service before the four of us lifted his coffin on to our shoulders, the church flooded with light. I knew it was him. Then it rained.

Sophy's dream, which mixes her family history with our grief and hers, is a powerful one. C. S. Lewis (Northern Irish historian of medieval and Renaissance literature, novelist, author of the Narnia stories, Christian theologian) says somewhere that there are big dreams that are given to certain people: Dante's dream of Beatrice, for example, out of which he fashioned *The Divine Comedy*, and, in particular, the magnificent interplanetary vision of interpenetrating light and music that is the astonishing Canto XIV of the *Paradiso*, foretelling the resurrection of the body to eternal life. Lewis goes on to say that such dreams happen with much less frequency now than was the case in the past. This I am sure is right, but such things still occur, especially at moments of crisis, or when a new direction is called for. Sophy's dream is a serious communication.

A few days after the funeral I dreamed of Egan myself. He was in a kind of obscurity, a fog, as in Sophy's vision. From this shade he stretched out his arms to hold me. I felt his embrace around my upper arms and shoulders, hugging me tightly in what felt like a farewell. And then, almost a year later, I dreamed of him again. I could see him clearly. It was as if he had gone through some change. He was younger than he was when he died, very like how he looked at his most handsome and heartbreaking, aged seventeen or so. Except that he was not pale and thin with the anorexia that afflicted him then. His skin was lustrous, even radiant and shining. His hair was thick and glossy, his eyes bright with the fire of energetic life. He looked at me and I could see that he knew who I was. Physically he had been renewed, transformed, but when he spoke his voice was sluggish and slurred. It was not the slurring that comes with drink, but it was as if he was learning, all over again, or trying to recall, the functions of speech. He was struggling to convey meaning. But then I understood what he was trying to say in the garbled language.

He told me I had spilled drink over him. It was alright, he said, but I had spilled drink on him. Which of course I had.

24

Clare Lake

In late summer 2006, while on holiday in Sardinia (once again guests of Pino's, but this time without Egan, who was getting ready to move into his new house in Coleraine), we sent a card to Ray Leonard in Claremorris, who had looked after Egan so well the year before.

When we got home we received a letter from Ray's wife Pauline. They had separated when Ray's bipolar mood swings became too much for them both: she distressed by his unpredictability, he racked by the effect his illness was having on her. Pauline told me that Ray had taken his own life the October before. This would have been the autumn of the year in which Ray, in his Christ-like manner, had helped Egan through some of his most difficult experiences.

At the bottom of the town of Claremorris, below the railway track, in a dip between the slight incline on which the town is built and the rising ground along which the road to Ballindine runs, is Clare Lake. This was once a boggy swamp that took the effluent from the bacon factory, but it has been reclaimed and holds stocks of bream, perch and pike. However, it is still a lonely place, retaining the atmosphere of the peatland mere it once was when the Celts built a crannóg, or man-made island, in the middle of its murky waters. Ray drowned himself in Clare Lake.

Sometimes I lie awake at night trying to imagine what Egan's last moments were like when he went under. Was there a sense of release? Or was it all just confusion? What was Ray's mind like as he went under? These are questions to which there are no answers. Today is 8 June 2008. I have been writing this now for over a year. Am I any closer to a sense that there is a meaning inscribed in the raw facts of the story of my son's life and death? I don't know; I have written enough.

25

Enough

No, I have not yet written enough. 'Enough' is a strange word. Look at it. It comes from the Anglo-Saxon, the Anglo-Saxon word itself deriving from an ancient Indo-European root, so it is a word that comes from the deepest stratum of the languages of Europe, the Middle East, the Indian sub-continent. It comes out of the sedimented layers of speech and writing, and there are almost identical words with the same meaning in Sanskrit and Old Frisian.

I want now to go to an astonishing use of the word in one of the most remarkable poems in English. The poem is by the Jesuit priest-poet Gerard Manley Hopkins, and it has a strange and daring title: 'That Nature is a Heraclitean Fire of the Comfort of the Resurrection'. This poem was read aloud in honour of Egan by Desmond Egan, himself a poet, at a tree-planting ceremony in the Kildare town of Monasterevin in the summer of 2007. The small ceremony took place during the Hopkins Summer School, which is held there every year. The tree, an oak, was planted in the Hopkins Memorial Garden on the banks of the River Barrow.

Hopkins? Monasterevin? Why? Hopkins, an English Anglican, converted to Catholicism under the influence of Cardinal John Henry Newman, and in 1884 became professor of Greek literature at University College, Dublin. Hopkins hated UCD, and Ireland depressed him. He found the grind of examining not just tedious and exhausting (he had to mark immense quantities of exam scripts), it threw him into panics of conscience. He would worry himself to agonised fatigue over fractions of percentages in the allocation of marks to clumsy pieces of Greek translation from students he had never met.

This nightmare of frantic worry and labour was made worse by the fact that he hated the nationalism that was rising in Ireland, especially amongst the newly emergent Catholic middle class. Monasterevin, through the friendship of two sisters who lived together in the town, became a haven and refuge, and he spent a number of Christmas breaks there in a house overlooking the river. Hence the (somewhat tenuous) connection with the town and the Hopkins Summer School that is held there every year.

In 2007 the Hopkins Society decided to dedicate that year's summer school to Egan's memory and to have a tree-planting ceremony in his honour in the memorial garden, where trees mark the contribution of distinguished past members and speakers, among them the sculptor James McKenna and the critic Hugh Kenner. This gesture took our breath away. Angela and I went down, as did Killian, Tiernan, Tiernan's girlfriend Lauren, Richard our son-in-law, Charlotte, Charlotte's mother and some other friends. A delegation.

The poem opens with a vastness combined with a startling set of specific evocations of the actuality of things: clouds, light, trees, the shadows that branches make on white-washed walls, leaves shivering in the light, the boisterous surges of the wind, mud, human footprints in dried pools. These details are gathered up into the powerful impulsive rush of the verse to evoke the fire that rages and drives variously through the energy that is in nature, that *is* nature. But then the poem turns into question, into a restless Jesuit interrogation, seeking truth. What of man? What of death? How soon, Hopkins mourns, the mark of man is gone. How completely, he says, a man's energy and his mental power are, 'in an unfathomable, all in an enormous dark/ Drowned'. Time, he goes on to say, beats man 'level'. Then full stop. Dead. The spirit is down, out. And now occurs what Geoffrey Hill has hailed as one of the 'greatest grammatical moments in nineteenth-century English poetry', what he calls an 'uncouth anacoluthon'. An anacoluthon is a shift in the grammar, a break in the syntax and the sense. Geoffrey Hill describes what Hopkins does here by saying, 'suddenly there bursts in an uncouth anacoluthon'. This is what happens: ' ... time beats level. Enough! The Resurrection,/ A heart's clarion! Away grief's grasping, joyless days, dejection./ Across my foundering deck shone/ A beacon, an eternal beam. Flesh fade and mortal trash/ Fall to the residuary worm; world's wildfire, leave but ash:/ In a flash, at a trumpet crash/ I am all at once what Christ is, since he was what I am, and/ This Jack, joke, poor potsherd, patch, matchwood, immortal diamond/ Is immortal diamond.'

This is a poetry of a weltering intensity carrying the highest charge of effort and feeling. It delivers the experience of the realisation of change, where joylessness and Coleridgean dejection can shift into the readiness to fight darkness and gloom that resurrection, as we experience it in our lives, is. This is poetry as a soldiery of courage: the Jesuits are known as 'miles Christi', the soldiers of Christ. But look again at what Hopkins writes. This shift happens in 'a flash'. There is, even in the strenuous exertion that Hopkins's verse becomes in this poem, a sense that this is only a momentary glimmer, a flash, but that there is much more to hope for.

The theologian H.A. Williams, in *True Resurrection*, quotes from William James, the philosopher-brother of the novelist Henry, to illustrate how even in fairly normal acts of perception there are present intimations, 'glimmers', that lie beyond the ability of words to capture. James writes as follows in *The Varieties of Religious Experience* (1902): 'Philosophy lives in words, but truth and fact well up into our lives in many ways that exceed verbal formulation. There is in the living act of perception always something that glimmers and twinkles and will not be caught and for which reflection comes too late.'

I have written at the end of the last chapter about my inability to think what may have been in Egan's mind or in the mind of Ray Leonard when they each, in their separate ways, went under. Ray's death was a suicide; Egan's was not. But what was Egan doing up at the Loughan that night? How did he get there? From the housing development, where he was in the company of his old school friend, to the ancient site of the Loughan is a distance of about one-and-a-half miles, a long way when you are drunk and on foot. After about half a mile the pavement ceases. From then on he would have been walking on the verge of the road, probably on the right-hand side, facing any oncoming traffic. Surely he must have known he was headed *away* from town, upriver? Did he mean to go to the Loughan, knowing there might have been a chance of drink there? What was he doing turning into the Clyde Bar at quarter past six earlier that evening and releasing the sequence of events that flowed from that single decision? He was in the grip of his addiction, of course, but there was, in his own words, 'something else'.

Egan's was a nature that burned with excess; he was truly a 'world's wildfire' in the words Hopkins uses that were read out on the banks of the Barrow. This excess of his was, amongst other things, an excess of love. He was capable of unremitting love. This wildfire pouring out of him was evident in all kinds of ways: animals came to him; small children were drawn to him (I will never forget the two little children on Brook Street saying what a good man my son was); plants that he potted up or put into earth just seemed to thrust themselves into growth. This excess of being, this readiness to love, to be inter-involved with the ways things are, is the sign of the artist, and perhaps too of the drunk. The way Egan involved himself with things is very like the way that a great painter becomes involved with the colours and textures, the light, the raggedness of a bunch of sunflowers in a vase, so that when we look at the Van Gogh 'Sunflowers' we are not looking at a painting that tries to capture the way that the flowers looked on a certain morning or afternoon. We are looking at a new thing, a something else, a resurrection of Van Gogh in the form of the flowers, and of the flowers in the mental and emotional uniqueness that is the self of that painter, all vibrating in the cascade of experience that colour becomes in the painting. The painting is, to paraphrase Beckett on James Joyce, not a description of something, flowers; it becomes a something other, a 'something else', an experience. A new life has arisen out of the elements that were there: a painter, paint, brushes, flowers, time, light, a table, a vase and who knows what else: bad breath, flickers of pain, sorrow, despair, rancour. A new life emerges from the interplay of these elements, and they are transformed in the process. The drunk wants to find a way of joining in with the process where life may transform itself, but unless he is an artist (and many artists are drunks, though it is far from being the case that many drunks are artists), he or she cannot make the shift in the relations of the elements to one another that is the intoxicating charge in great poetry, great painting.

When Egan joined the waters of the Bann, there is a sense in which he was smashing through the indifference and obduracy of the world to become at one with its cold and beautiful flow. The impulse is of a kind that drove through Van Gogh as he sought immersion in the yellowness of the flowers, an act of unification we can see and feel in the painting. Egan was not an artist. He was not that kind of showman. He chose life, which, for him, involved such an intensity as to transform life into death.

I have no doubt but that Egan is in a place of resurrection; but I am also certain that nothing can be known of that until our current mental apparatus is no more. St Paul writes in his first letter to the Corinthians that when he first came to Corinth he was determined to make no pretence of knowing anything more than this: Jesus Christ and Him crucified. There is no need for anything more because everything flows from this basic fact. There was a person called Christ who was crucified, and in his death is our resurrection. Christ is the something else that glimmers at the edge of the human. No need for big speeches, straining rhetoric: the miraculous resides in the human, in death itself, even ignominious death. How little, St Paul says, we know of ourselves, of what we are; how much less can we know of the mystery of the world which constantly changes and renews itself. And then he quotes, altering it crucially to shift the emphasis to love, a text from Isaiah the prophet: ' ... as it is written, Eye hath not seen, nor ear heard, neither have entered into the heart of man, the things which God hath prepared for them that love him.'

26

A Message

On the night of 29 October 2007 I had one of those serious dreams
that come from time to time as a fortification of the spirit. I am not
that frequently blessed with such gifts, but occasionally they do
arrive, as if to remind me that a larger pattern exists which contains
our distresses and miseries. In the dream the German poet Rainer
Maria Rilke, who died in 1926, speaks to me and says the following:
'The challenge is to avoid, in a world so full of mystery, endless
sorrow, memory, lamentation.' I notice, as I write this conclusion to
my attempt to convey something of the hope of resurrection, that
the date is 29 October 2008, exactly a year since Rilke made his
blessed intervention.

Coleraine, Northern Ireland
Leamagowra, Donegal
Sassari, Sardinia
2007 – 2011
Revised and rewritten, Coleraine, February 2011.